The Shelbys Need Help!

THE SHELBYS

NEED HELP!

A Choose-Your-Own-Solutions
Guidebook for Parents

Dr. Ken West

Little
Imp
Books

Impact Publishers, Inc.
ATASCADERO, CALIFORNIA

ATTENTION ORGANIZATIONS AND CORPORATIONS:
This book is available at quantity discounts on bulk purchases for educational, business, or sales promotional use. For further information, please contact Impact Publishers, P.O. Box 6016, Atascadero, CA 93423-6016, Phone: 1-800-246-7228, e-mail: sales@impactpublishers.com

Library of Congress Cataloging-in-Publication Data

West, G. Kenneth.
The Shelbys need help! : a choose-your-own-solutions guidebook for parents
    / Ken West.
        p. cm.
"Includes the Shelbys A-Z parenting guide with case examples."
Includes bibliographical references.
ISBN 1-886230-16-1 (alk. paper)
    1. Child rearing--Miscellanea. 2. Parenting--Miscellanea. 3. Parent and child--Miscellanea. I. Title.

HQ769 .W47 2000
649'.1--dc21   00-036956

Publisher's Note
This publication is designed to provide accurate and authoritative information in regard to the subject matter covered. It is sold with the understanding that the publisher is not engaged in rendering psychological, legal, or other professional services. If expert assistance or counseling is needed, the services of a competent professional should be sought.

Impact Publishers and colophon are registered trademarks of Impact Publishers, Inc.

Illustrations by Bryan Fitz, Lynchburg, Virginia
Cover design by John Magee, San Luis Obispo, California
Printed in the United States of America on acid-free paper
Published by ***Impact Publishers, Inc.***
POST OFFICE BOX 6016
ATASCADERO, CALIFORNIA 93423-6016
www.impactpublishers.com

Acknowledgments

So many people to thank! Mrs. Betty Leighton, a friend and mentor since I was 18, gave invaluable help in the creation of *The Shelbys*. Bryan Fitz brought *The Shelbys* to life with his illustrations. Bryan won a Shelbys' Art Contest sponsored by Central Virginia's newspaper, *The News & Advance,* for whom I have written a column for 15 years.

My wife Patty remains my most constant source of inspiration and encouragement. And, of course, readers will see the influence of our three children: Patrick (a Duke graduate, now at the University of Virginia's Medical School), Emily (a student at Vanderbilt) and Dustin (a student at Yale).

Patty's mother, Mrs. Annette Leight, and her five sisters, one brother and cherished in-laws have always encouraged my writing: Molly, Betty (Bob), Missy (Charlie), Sally (Gary), Edwin (Meredith), Peggy (Paul) and their children. My sister Becky and her husband Dwight have been constant supporters.

Lynchburg College, where I have taught for 24 years, and LC's Center for Family Education provided economic support. At LC, special thanks go to Dr. Ed Polloway, Dr. Tom Tiller, Dr. Steve Nielsen and the faculty of the counseling program. Dr. David Smith, Dr. Bill Robinson and Ron Wellman became constant inspirations.

Most importantly, I thank the many men and women of NASAP (North American Society of Adlerian Psychology) who tirelessly support parents through their research, writing and teaching. NASAP's influence can be seen in the ideas that support such exceptional parent education programs as "Active Parenting Today" and "STEP" (Systematic Training for Effective Parenting).

Finally, thanks to my publisher, Bob Alberti, and the staff at Impact, who selected, nurtured and published a very "different" manuscript.

Contents

The Shelbys Need Help!

Choose-Your-Own-Solutions Guidebook for Parents

It All Began ...

When Mom and Dad Shelby moved to Central City ten years ago. They believed the town would be the perfect place to raise perfect children. Then the three Shelby Children were born. At least Mom and Dad Shelby still believe that Central City is ideal, but their kids! No one ever warned them that their children would make a herd of starving pit bulls seem self-disciplined and cooperative.

William (age nine), Wendy (age seven), and Wally (age almost five) show flashes of cuteness, of course. But each bolt of charm seems trifling compared to their never-ending attempts to defy Mom and Dad Shelby at home and to humiliate them in public. As an architect, Dad Shelby designs skyscrapers that will endure hurricane-force winds, but he confesses, "I can't take them on a simple trip to the zoo without having the afternoon collapse into bickering, badgering and backbiting. The animals run to their caves when they see us coming."

Mom Shelby thinks Dad should loosen up. "If you believe *our* kids are bad, you should see the ones I teach at Longfellow Middle School," the part-time teacher reminds him. "There are children out there who make ours look like — well, make them look better, anyway."

That would be news to the Carlsons, the Shelbys' neighbors. After William collected a bag of empty jars and broke them one by one against the rim of the Carlsons' fishpond, the neighbors installed a seven-foot chain link fence designed to keep the Shelby wildlife out. That was two years ago. Since then, the Carlsons have blamed the Shelby kids for the mysterious death of their cat, the frequent vandalism of their ceramic deer herd and the occasional torturing of their pet dog Liberty. Now, the Carlsons routinely clip out columns by parenting experts and announcements for parent study classes and tape them to the Shelbys' front door.

The Carlsons' suggestions aren't well received.

"I don't need help raising my children," screams Dad Shelby. "All I need is a ten-foot rod and the courage to use it."

"You've already tried that, dear," Mom Shelby reminds him. "Besides, what our children need is a little more love and understanding. A gentle hug settles the most savage beast." And so it goes within the Shelby Wildlife Preserve. In a fit of rage, Dad Shelby recently demanded: "Who's in charge here, anyway?" The answer is clear: William, Wendy and Wally.

The Shelbys need help. If you turn this page, you will become Mom and Dad Shelbys' consultant. As their advisor, you will counsel them on the choices to make in some of parenting's most challenging situations.

I warn you: Don't continue blithely! Being a parent, particularly to the Shelby kids, is never as easy as experts or childless relatives may lead you to believe. *Continue at your own risk!*

I see that you didn't heed my warning. Oh, well, come along. You're just in time to hear the alarm that begins an ordinary day at the Shelby home. But put on a mental seat belt. Your sanity will be at risk: there's turbulence ahead!

SCENE 1

The six-thirty alarm sounds, but only William and Wendy are asleep. Dad left early for a breakfast meeting, and Wally awoke thirty minutes ago, ready to play. Mom Shelby puts toys beside Wally's bed to distract him in the morning. Nevertheless, Wally prefers company and usually manages to roust Mom Shelby from bed.

Soon after the alarm rings, William climbs out of bed to ready himself for the 7:40 school bus that carries him and Wendy to Lincoln Elementary School. As William puts on his clothes, he notices that his shoes are missing.

"Mom, Wally hid my shoes again!" he yells.

"I did not. He's lying," responds Wally in a tone that reflects his lack of certainty about whether he took them or not.

Mom marches into William's room. "Your shoes are right in the bathroom where you left them. If you would just look for things instead of yelling at people, then you'd be ready for school on time.

As Mom returns to the kitchen, she calls over her shoulder, "It's time for breakfast. William! Wally! Wendy! . . . Wendy! Where's Wendy? Don't tell me. Not again. That girl stays up so late looking at her books."

Mom rushes into Wendy's room to discover that Wendy is in a deep sleep.

If you believe Mom Shelby should ...

*... pull Wendy out of bed and make sure her feet are
on the floor* .... **Turn to Scene 2**

*... say, "Wendy, this is your first and last wake-up call.
You're on your own now,"* .... **Turn to Scene 3**

*... say, "I know how tired you are, Wendy. I'm pleased that you like to look at
your books at night, so I allowed you to sleep a little longer.
But now it's time to get up,"* .... **Turn to Scene 4**

SCENE 2

Put both feet on the floor *now*," shouts Mom Shelby, reaching for her daughter.

"Keep your hands off me, Mom!" yells an exhausted-looking Wendy.

Mom retorts, "You know better than to go back to sleep. Now I'm going to make sure you're up. Put your feet *on the floor!*"

Mom pulls harder on Wendy's arm. In retaliation, Wendy screams one of her favorite air raid howls that echoes through the house. By the end of her shriek, William and Wally arrive at the door to join the excitement. "Whack her, Mom — Wendy's hurting our ears," urges Wally.

"Stay out of this!" threatens Mom Shelby.

Feeling attacked on all fronts, Wendy sits on the side of her bed, her face revealing the last fragment of human righteousness. Finally she proclaims, "I'm not eating breakfast or going to school."

If you believe Mom Shelby should ...

> *... say, "O.K. If you can't cooperate, I'll have to help dress you*
> *and escort you to breakfast myself,"* .... **Turn to Scene 5**

> *... say, "I know you're upset. If you pull yourself together and get dressed,*
> *I'll make your favorite blueberry pancakes,"* .... **Turn to Scene 9**

> *... say, "That's up to you. I don't have time to play games*
> *right now,"* .... **Turn to Scene 11**

SCENE 3

Mom Shelby wakes Wendy up and leaves her on her own.

Meanwhile, William prepares for school. Last night, he had returned all of his school materials to his backpack in order to be ready this morning. After changing his mind several times about which shirt to wear, William chooses his YMCA basketball shirt, grabs his backpack, and charges past Wendy's room.

But wait a minute! There's Wendy, asleep *again*. William can't resist: "Good-bye, Wendy. I'm on the way to catch the school bus. You have nine minutes."

Wendy darts out of bed, looks at her clock and panics. As she hurries to put on her jeans, she loses her balance and crumbles to the floor. Tears flow as she frantically dresses, grabs a few of her school materials and runs to the kitchen.

"Mom, I'm late. Why didn't you wake me up? Now I don't have time to eat. I'll probably starve to death before lunch," scolds the feisty one as she heads out the door to catch the bus.

If you believe Mom Shelby should ...

> *... say nothing and allow Wendy to leave the house
> without intervention,* .... **Turn to Scene 16**

> *... grab Wendy's arm and set the record straight, saying, "It was your decision
> to go back to sleep. Now you take the consequences,"* .... **Turn to Scene 17**

> *... try to make peace by offering to drive Wendy to school after she
> eats breakfast,* .... **Turn to Scene 89**

SCENE 4

Mom Shelby awakens Wendy, saying, "I'm pleased you like to read your books at night, so I allowed you to sleep a little longer. But now it's time to get up."

Wendy opens her eyes, and Mom Shelby leaves to supervise things in the kitchen.

After a hurried breakfast, Mom Shelby rushes William out the door and turns her attention to helping Wally dress. But wait a minute! Where's Wendy?

Mom streaks to Wendy's room to discover that Wendy has fallen to sleep *again*.

"Wendy, please get up! You only have nine minutes before the bus comes," urges Mom.

"Mom, I can't make it! And we're going on a field trip today. Can you take me to school this one time? I promise I'll be ready in time tomorrow," pleads Wendy.

If you believe Mom Shelby should ...

... say, "I will take you this time. But it will be the last time. Now get ready, and be in the car in exactly fifteen minutes," .... **Turn to Scene 13**

... say, "I will drive you, but it will cost you one-half of your week's allowance for cab fare," .... **Turn to Scene 10**

Mom Shelby strides toward Wendy, intending to help her dress.

"Don't you dare touch me!" yells Wendy.

Determined, Mom Shelby grabs Wendy's jeans from the closet and marches toward her. "I gave you a chance to do it yourself and you were too lazy. Now we're going to do it my way."

Wendy strikes her hand out and catches Mom Shelby flush on the cheek.

If you believe Mom Shelby should ...

... slap Wendy with authority to show her who is boss, ... **Turn to Scene 6**

... set the record straight by saying, "After all I've done for you, how can you treat me this way? You're grounded for a month, young lady," ...... **Turn to Scene 7**

9

SCENE 6

Mom Shelby strikes Wendy, warning, "The Shelbys don't hit people. Don't ever slap me again!"

Out of desperation, Wendy pushes Mom Shelby. Surprised, Mom Shelby loses her balance and falls to the floor.

Wendy runs from the room, screaming, "I hate you."

Mom Shelby replies, "You're about to get the beating of your life." As Mom looks up in the doorway, she sees Wally looking at her, his face filled with terror.

Second Chance! Turn to Scene 1

But first, see **Power Struggles** (page 237) and
Power Struggles Case Study 1:
The Shelbys Don't Hit! in the *A–Z Parenting Guide* (page 238).

SCENE 7

Mom Shelby storms out of the room feeling angry and hurt.

Also feeling angry and hurt, Wendy slips her clothes on and sneaks toward the front door. As she slinks through the doorway, she notices Mom Shelby's prized antique vase, given to the family by Great Grandmother Shelby.

Following a slight flick of her wrist, the vase topples to the floor, smashing into pieces.

Hearing the crash, Mom shelby runs toward the front door and stands over the broken family heirloom. Her heart sinks as she wonders, "How could one of my children treat me this way after all I have done for them?"

If you believe Mom Shelby should ...

*... chase Wendy and keep her from getting away
with this atrocity,* . . . . **Turn to Scene 8**

... call a family therapist and ask for an appointment, ... **Turn to Scene 91**

SCENE 8

Mom Shelby runs out of the house to pursue Wendy. She spies Wendy at the bus stop talking with several friends. The students warn Wendy that her mom is approaching.

Just as Mom Shelby arrives, Wendy darts across the street.

William screams, "Watch out!"

Too late! A driver hits his brakes, and the car skids toward Wendy. Freezing, Wendy grimaces, waiting for impact. Miraculously, the car stops within six inches of her. Terrified, Mom Shelby runs toward her frightened daughter.

Seeing her, Wendy yells, "Leave me alone!" and runs across the street, disappearing into the woods.

Second Chance! Turn to Scene 1

But first, see **Revenge** (page 245) and the **Revenge Case Study: Massacre at Broken Vase** in the *A–Z Parenting Guide* (page 245).

SCENE 9

Mom Shelby returns to the kitchen and takes the blueberry pancakes out of the freezer. She's more than a little annoyed to spend extra time fixing breakfast when she should be studying her lesson plans, but the effort seems worth it. Anything to calm the family storms.

Finally, Wendy lumbers into the kitchen, but she's not dressed for school. In fact, she's still in her nightgown and slippers.

If you believe Mom Shelby should say, "You will never make it to the bus stop on time now, but . . ."

... *"I will take you this one time. I'm warning you though: this better never happen again or you'll be in serious trouble,"* .... **Turn to Scene13**

... *"I will take you this morning, but I'll have to make up the time I miss from work after school. So I will not be able to take you to dance lessons today,"* .... **Turn to Scene 10**

SCENE 10

Wendy cannot believe her mother's heartless declaration and cries, "You know that's not fair!"

Swiftly, Wendy dresses, grabs an apple out of the fruit bowl, and runs to gather her school books. Without saying as much as a "Good-bye, Mom," Wendy streaks from the house, slamming the door behind her.

Mom Shelby smiles to herself, but soon her contentment fades. "Oh, my, it's late! I've got to have Wally in preschool in ten minutes."

Running toward Wally's room, Mom Shelby discovers him playing with his toys. The clothes Mom Shelby laid out for him lie scattered on the floor.

If you believe that Mom Shelby should ...

... insist on dressing Wally so she won't be late, ... **Turn to Scene 31**

... inform him that they will leave in six minutes no matter what condition he is in, ... **Turn to Scene 23**

... give him a smack on the rear to get his attention, then hurry him along, ... **Turn to Scene 18**

SCENE 11

"That's up to you. I don't have time to play games right now," declares Mom Shelby as she leaves the room.

Wendy dallies around in her bedroom for a few minutes, waiting for something interesting to happen. But William is busy organizing his collections and Wally is fighting off imaginary bandits attempting to invade his room. Wendy hears the sound of dishes being put away as Mom Shelby finishes cleaning up the breakfast mess.

Wendy dresses and goes into the kitchen to investigate. Slumping into a chair beside Mom Shelby, Wendy too innocently inquires, "What's for breakfast?"

If you believe that Mom Shelby should respond ...

> ... *"We've all eaten. Fix your own, but remember that you have six or*
> *seven minutes to catch the bus,"* .... **Go on to Scene 12**

> ... *"You missed breakfast, and you'll probably miss the bus too.*
> *I'll give you a ride today, but from now on when you miss the bus*
> *you'll have to find your own way to school,"* .... **Turn to Scene 89**

SCENE 12

Panicked that the school bus will leave her, Wendy gobbles down some leftovers from the night before, gathers her books and runs out the door. On her way out she screams, "Mom, you've gotta wake me up earlier. How can I be ready on time?"

Mom Shelby's anger flashes, but for once she holds her tongue. After all, she finally stood up to Wendy. She should celebrate.

As Mom Shelby begins to ready herself for school, she notices that the house seems too quiet. *Oh no! Where is Wally?*

After a short search, Mom Shelby discovers Wally playing on the floor with his toys. In fact, toys litter the room from one side to the other. To make matters worse, Wally's carefully laid out clothes have been tossed to the floor.

"Wally!" Mom exclaims. "We must leave in six minutes."

If you believe Mom Shelby should ...

> ... *insist on dressing Wally so she won't be late,* .... **Turn to Scene 31**

> ... *say, "It's up to you whether or not you dress for preschool.*
> *One way or the other, we will leave in six minutes,"* .... **Turn to Scene 23**

> ... *give Wally a spank on the rear to get his attention and*
> *to hurry him along,* .... **Turn to Scene 18**

SCENE 13

Feeling worse and worse about promising her crafty daughter a ride, Mom Shelby begins to rush Wendy to get ready to leave. After all, once she drops Wendy at school, Mom Shelby must return home with Wally to prepare him for preschool. But as you would guess, the more Mom Shelby pushes, the "more slower" goes her daughter.

After enough prodding to hustle an entire herd of cattle into a boxcar, Mom finally shoves Wally and Wendy into the car.

As they approach the school, Wendy asks, "Did anyone remember to bring my permission slip for the class field trip?"

Mom Shelby's heart sinks. She can still see the form where she left it on top of Wendy's backpack. What did Wendy do with it? Mom Shelby hopelessly wonders.

If you believe that Mom Shelby should ...

... say, "I'm sorry, Wendy, I cannot take you home. Next time maybe you'll have everything organized better," .... **Turn to Scene 16**

... realize how important the field trip is to Wendy and return for the form, ... **Turn to Scene 15**

... say, "We should have communicated better. It's my fault too. But I'm too rushed to return home," .... **Turn to Scene 14**

"I simply will not be late for my classes, Wendy. I'm sorry, but I just won't," explains Mom Shelby.

"That's not fair. You know how much I'm looking forward to this field trip. I'll be the only one not able to go. They'll make me sit in with another stupid class. Please, Mom! Please!" pleads Wendy.

Obviously upset, Mom holds her ground. "Dear, if there were any way that I could go back, you know I would. I'm so sorry. We should have communicated better."

Wendy gets out of the car, slams the door and begins to cry loudly. Mom sighs. She considers driving on, but cannot bear to see Wendy so unhappy. Mom Shelby gets out of her car and walks toward Wendy to comfort her. As she reaches Wendy, the youngster gives Mom Shelby a kick in the shins. "You're not fair! I hate you," Wendy screams.

Mom looks up to see the teacher on bus duty shaking her head in disgust. Mom Shelby feels hurt and humiliated. Wendy Shelby, ironically, shares the same feelings.

Second Chance! Turn to Scene 13

But first, see **Permissiveness** (page 232) and **Permissiveness Case Study 1: Who Is the Real Monster?** in the *A–Z Parenting Guide* (page 233).

SCENE 15

Mom Shelby begins to return home in haste. Every second of the trip, she abuses herself. *Why didn't I refuse? What went wrong? Why does everyone always take advantage of me?*

Preoccupied, Mom Shelby doesn't see the stop sign. Too bad for her that the police officer's concentration is better. Being given a ticket along a well-travelled road, Mom Shelby feels as if her entire world is caving in. Suddenly a horn honks. She sees her neighbors, the Carlsons, driving by. Oh my! That means there will be more clippings taped to the front door. "Why does everything happen to me?" Mom Shelby mutters as tears begin to flow.

Second Chance! Turn to Scene 13

But first, see **Natural Consequences** (page 225)
and **Natural Consequences Case Study 1:**
A Ticket for Your Troubles in the *A–Z Parenting Guide* (page 226).

SCENE 16

As Wendy storms away, Mom Shelby reflects, "Sometimes parents do the right thing and they still don't feel good about it. I know what I did was best for Wendy and for me, but why don't I feel better?"

Mom has little time to seek an answer. She needs to finish dressing, review her lesson plans (as if there were ever time!) and ferry Wally to school. Wally!

Suddenly Mom Shelby realizes that she's lost track of Wally. Running to his bedroom, she worries about the trouble he may have initiated.

As she enters his bedroom, she sees toys scattered from one end of the room to the other.

"I'm playing, and none of my figures wanted to be left in the toy box," explains Wally.

Although the mess irritates Mom Shelby, she's more disturbed that Wally has not started to dress.

If you believe Mom Shelby should ...

> *... insist on dressing Wally so she won't be late,* .... **Turn to Scene 31**

> *... say, "It's up to you whether or not you dress for school.*
> *One way or the other, we will leave in six minutes,"* .... **Turn to Scene 23**

> *... give Wally a little whack on the rear to get his attention*
> *and to hurry him along,* .... **Turn to Scene 18**

19

SCENE 17

Mom Shelby catches up to Wendy and announces, "Young lady, you decided to go back to bed, not me. You were the one who was irresponsible. Now I expect you to straighten up. Who do you think you are, anyway?"

Somehow Mom Shelby knew she shouldn't have asked. Wendy, of course, offers an answer Mom Shelby doesn't wish to hear: "I think I'm the daughter of the meanest witch in the city. How can you be so horrible to me?"

Being quicker than her befuddled mother, Wendy flees from the Shelby house and runs to the bus stop — never hearing Mom Shelby's reply.

Feeling absolutely defeated, Mom Shelby wants to reflect about what went wrong and what should be done when the next crisis arises. But she realizes that her time is running out. Mom Shelby's work begins in less than thirty minutes.

"Maybe," Mom Shelby thinks, "Wally will be dressed and ready to go to school for once. Something has to go right."

No such luck. Mom Shelby rounds the corner only to see Wally surrounded by tiny balls of modeling clay. Worse, he's still in his pajamas. His clothes, once folded nicely on his bed, have been tossed to the floor.

If you believe Mom Shelby should ...

... insist on dressing Wally so she won't be late, ... **Turn to Scene 31**

*... say, "It's up to you whether or not you dress for school.
One way or the other, we will leave in six minutes,"* .... **Turn to Scene 23**

*... give him a little whack on the rear to get his attention
and to hurry him along,* .... **Turn to Scene 18**

SCENE 18

"I don't want to dress now!" pleads Wally.

"We all do lots of things in life we don't want to do," responds Mom Shelby, becoming increasingly exasperated.

"I don't care. I want to play. Get out of my room!" commands Wally.

The young rebel's tone becomes the proverbial last straw. Mom Shelby charges toward Wally and gives him a whack on the rear to remind him who's in charge.

Wally cries more in protest than in pain. His shrieks become louder and louder, then change to angry moping. Wally throws himself on his bed and sobs.

Mom Shelby knows that Wally's feelings are hurt. But also she notices that he is not getting dressed.

If you believe Mom Shelby should say ...

> ... *"If you think you have something to cry about now, just see what will happen if you're not dressed in five minutes,"* ......**Turn to Scene 19**

> ... *"I know I hurt your feelings, but you need to understand my feelings too,"* .... **Turn to Scene 22**

SCENE 19

Mom warns Wally that he hasn't seen anything yet!

Wally remains on his bed, weeping. Nevertheless, he keeps an eye glued on Mom Shelby. Tension mounts. With every passing second, Mom Shelby's anger rises.

Wally knows that he's playing a risky game. As much as he enjoys seeing his mother overheat and lose control, Wally wants to avoid one of Mom Shelby's super-spankings. The gamble seems worthwhile: Wally emits a slow, mournful cry.

Bad decision!

Mom Shelby rips into Wally! Her hand strikes several hard blows before Wally can budge from his bed.

Shocked, Wally responds with dazed silence.

After the volley of whacks concludes, Mom Shelby notices a peculiar look spread over Wally's face. Now, she becomes the startled one.

"Mom, I wet my pants," confesses Wally.

If you believe Mom Shelby should ...

... express her outrage and show him who is in charge, ... **Turn to Scene 20**

... offer to help him clean up and dress, ... **Turn to Scene 21**

SCENE 20

Outraged and worn down by the events of the morning, Mom Shelby grabs Wally by the arms and squeezes it hard.

"You have to realize who's in charge in this house and begin to follow my directions," Mom Shelby yells.

"You're hurting me!" cries Wally.

This time Wally's voice alarms Mom Shelby. She releases him, but Wally's no longer crying. The youngster slumps to the floor holding his arm. Red marks on his arm are clearly visible.

Mom Shelby's heart breaks. *How could I have done this?* she ponders. With her whole body filling with grief and panic, Mom Shelby says anxiously, "Wally, I didn't mean to hurt you."

Wally looks away. Mom feels grief-stricken. *I just wish I could replay this entire scene,* she sighs.

Second Chance! Turn to Scene 31

But first, see **Dressing** (page 200) and the **Dressing Case Study: Wally in the Morning** in the *A–Z Parenting Guide* (page 201).

SCENE 21

Mom Shelby realizes that her morning is growing worse and that she has wandered down a destructive path. "Sometimes," Mom Shelby thinks, "it's just best to admit that I've lost control and that we need to start over."

Mom Shelby explains, "Wally, sometimes when you don't cooperate with me, I feel frustrated and angry. I don't mean to hurt you. I'm sorry." After a moment of silence, she adds, "I need your help. Can we work together?"

Wally nods his assent and walks to the bathroom. He doesn't ask for help and manages to take care of himself. When Wally finishes, Mom Shelby asks whether or not he can finish dressing without her assistance. Wally nods his head affirmatively, and Mom begins to prepare for school.

Turn to Scene 88

SCENE 22

"When you don't dress for school, I get really upset because I might be late for my job. If I lose my job, we won't have enough money to do the things we all enjoy. When you dress on time and help me, I feel very good. Wouldn't you rather have a happy mom than a sad mom?" Mom Shelby inquires.

Wally seems to understand. He goes to Mom Shelby and wraps his arms around her neck.

Mom Shelby thinks, *Talking always works out so much better.* Warm feelings rush through Mom and the moment becomes a special one for Wally and Mom Shelby.

If you believe Mom Shelby should say …

… *"Dress quickly and we'll pick up a snack
on the way to school,"* . . . . **Turn to Scene 32**

… *"Dress on your own. Call me if you have any trouble.
We'll need to leave in six minutes,"* . . . . **Go on to Scene 23**

SCENE 23

Mom Shelby explains, "I'm going to leave you on your own to dress. We're going to leave in six minutes."

Mom leaves the room. But she journeys no more than ten steps before she hears, "Mom, I need your help."

Irritated, Mom Shelby returns to Wally's room. She sees him sitting on the bed, still in his pajamas. He has put on his socks but nothing else.

"These socks don't feel right. I need another pair," entreats Wally.

"There is absolutely nothing wrong with these socks. You went with me when we picked them out," replies Mom Shelby.

"But Mom, they just don't feel right," insists Wally.

Carefully, Mom adjusts Wally's socks to make sure they fit him correctly. Nothing seems to be wrong, but she fiddles with them hoping that her effort will satisfy him.

No such luck.

"They still feel funny," complains Wally.

If you believe Mom Shelby should say …

… *"I'm sorry that they feel funny, but I cannot help you.
Find some different socks if you wish. But we're leaving
in five minutes,"* . . . . **Turn to Scene 25**

… *"There is nothing wrong with these socks. Put them on and
quit complaining,"* . . . . **Turn to Scene 24**

SCENE 24

Mom Shelby insists that Wally wear the socks. "There's absolutely nothing wrong with your socks," she protests.

"I'm not going to wear these awful things!" shouts Wally.

To emphasize his point, he throws his socks to the floor, then sits on the edge of his bed pouting.

Mom Shelby has travelled several miles past the annoyed exit. She picks up Wally's socks and begins to force them over his feet. In retaliation, Wally begins to flail his legs.

Outraged, Mom Shelby yells, "You're acting like a spoiled brat. Straighten up this second!"

His feelings hurt, Wally sprawls out on his bed, crying pathetically.

If you believe Mom Shelby should ...

*... say, "If you think that you can act like this, then you have
another think coming,"* .... **Turn to Scene 20**

... change her tack and share her feelings with Wally, ... **Turn to Scene 30**

SCENE 25

"We're leaving in five minutes. Find some different socks if you wish," suggests Mom Shelby.

Mom leaves the room and Wally fiddles with his socks again. Finally, he decides to ransack his drawer to find a better pair. Soon he discovers the appropriate socks and slides them on.

Somewhat miffed at being left on his own, Wally listlessly slips into his shirt and pants. Then he begins to explore his room, mounting a search for his missing sneakers.

After a brief search, he discovers his shoes under the bed where he threw them the night before. Then he remembers, "My shoes got soaked when I fell into the Carlsons' stupid fish pond."

Turn to Scene 26

SCENE 26

"**M**om! Come here. It's an emergency!" shouts Wally.

Mom Shelby recognizes his tone of voice and isn't pleased. This particular tone generally signals that Wally's problem is about to become Mom Shelby's problem.

Entering Wally's room, Mom Shelby inquires, "What is it now, Wally?"

"My stupid shoes are wet and my old tennis shoes are too small to wear," he complains.

"Then you'll have to wear your dress shoes," announces Mom after evaluating Wally's options.

"No way!" shouts Wally. "I hate my dress shoes. I'm not going to wear them. I hate shoes with shoestrings!"

If you believe Mom Shelby should say ...

... *"You must wear your dress shoes anyway, because it's the only option,"* ....**Turn to Scene 29**

... *"You can wear your wet shoes, tennis shoes or dress shoes, Wally. It doesn't matter to me,"* ....**Turn to Scene 27**

SCENE 27

Mom Shelby leaves the choice of shoes up to Wally. The youngster cringes under the prospect of wearing the one pair of shoes that fits and is dry — dress shoes!

"That's not fair, Mom! I'll be the only kid in the world wearing dress shoes. Everyone will laugh at me. Can't you put my wet shoes in the dryer?" pleads Wally.

"I'm sorry, Wally, but we just don't have time to dry your shoes," Mom Shelby replies.

"But it's not fair," proclaims Wally.

If you believe Mom Shelby should say ...

... *"I'm sorry, Wally. We don't have time to dry your shoes,*
but if you hurry we can drop by the Quicky Mart for a snack
on the way to school," .... **Turn to Scene 32**

... *"Lots of things aren't fair. We need to go to the car,"* .... **Turn to Scene 28**

SCENE 28

Wally takes his wet shoes and his dress shoes to the car. He tries on one wet shoe, but then removes it. "Now, my sock is wet," the youngster complains.

Mom says nothing and keeps driving toward the preschool.

Finally, Wally manages to slip into his dress shoes. He refuses to tie them. Finished, he folds his arms over his chest and scowls. Wally is unaccustomed to not getting his way.

Mom Shelby knows better than to try to stop Wally's pouting. Instead, she turns up the volume on the radio and drives on.

When they arrive at the preschool, Mom reaches over to kiss Wally good-bye, but he's too quick — he opens the door and rushes out.

Mom Shelby wishes him a good day. In reply, Wally slams the door.

Pleased that she did not accept Wally's problem as her own, Mom drives toward her school. "I wish I felt better," she reflects. "But I'm pleased that I have a teachers' meeting this afternoon and Dad Shelby will be home before me!"

As she arrives at her school, Mom Shelby looks forward to a break in the family soap opera. "After a morning like this, work will seem like a vacation."

Turn to Scene 45

SCENE 29

"**Y**ou can't make me wear these dumb-looking shoes," challenges Wally.

"You'd better believe I can make you wear them. There is no other choice," rebuts Mom Shelby.

To reinforce her viewpoint, Mom Shelby rushes toward Wally. Knowing that he's about to lose the battle, Wally dives onto the floor and tosses a ferocious temper tantrum.

Mom watches as Wally's hands and feet flail against the floor. As the youngster's screams escalate, Mom Shelby must make another decision.

If you believe Mom Shelby should ...

> *... grab Wally and let him know once and for all that he cannot
> act like this in the Shelby home,* .... **Turn to Scene 20**
>
> *... quietly walk out the door and say nothing to Wally,* .... **Turn to Scene 41**

SCENE 30

"I feel frustrated and rushed, Wally. I know I hurt your feelings and I'm sorry. I really need your help, and you're a good helper. This morning I'll let you dress by yourself. Find a pair of socks that you like. Call me if you need help," explains a calmer Mom Shelby.

Wally feels good and bad. He is pleased that Mom Shelby asked for his help and will allow him to dress on his own. But he misses Mom Shelby's involvement. Wally loves Mom Shelby and he wants to enjoy her attention whenever possible.

This is not fun, Wally complains to himself. He opens his clothes drawer and shuffles through his socks. Finally, he discovers a pair that seems acceptable.

After putting on the rest of his clothes, Wally begins to search for his shoes. He discovers them partially hidden beneath his chest-of-drawers.

"Oh no!" Wally yells. "I forgot that my shoes got wet last night when I was hopping over those dumb rain puddles."

Turn to Scene 26

SCENE 31

"Wally, I need to help you dress today. I'm in too much of a hurry to wait for you," explains Mom Shelby, desperately hoping that he will accept her offer.

No such luck.

"Mom, I'll do it myself," Wally demands autonomously.

Just the response Mom Shelby feared!

What shall I do now? Mom Shelby wonders. Hurriedly, she reviews possible solutions as the clock ticks off the precious seconds remaining before her school day begins.

If you believe Mom Shelby should say ...

... *"I know that you can dress yourself. But it will be faster*
if I help you. In fact, if I help we'll have time to stop
at the Quicky Mart for a snack," .... **Turn to Scene 32**

... *"We just don't have time, Wally. I am going to have to help you*
this morning," .... **Turn to Scene 43**

... *"O.K., you dress. But let's play a game. I'm going to dress too.*
Let's see who finishes first!" .... **Turn to Scene 35**

SCENE 32

Mom Shelby doesn't feel pleased as she drives toward the Quicky Mart. *Why do I always have to bribe Wally to do what he should do anyway?* she contemplates.

Before she can answer the question, they arrive at the Quicky Mart and enter the store.

Wally races through the aisles and comes back clutching two candy bars and a giant pack of chewing gum.

"You can't have all of that, Wally. Choose one thing," orders Mom.

"That's not fair. You didn't tell me I could only have one thing!" retorts Wally. "Let me have two things, just this once."

"Absolutely not!" counters Mom Shelby, sticking to her guns.

Wally huffs up in that special way that promises public humiliation for Mom Shelby will soon follow.

He returns to the candy section and throws his three choices back on the shelf. Then he sits on the floor in front of the candy and scrutinizes each selection.

"We don't have time for you to study each piece of candy!" announces Mom.

Wally doesn't say anything. He selects another candy bar, then tosses it back on the shelf.

Mom Shelby has suffered enough.

She grabs Wally's arm and exhorts, "We've got to hurry!"

At the precise moment when Mom Shelby touches Wally, he screams and sprawls across the floor. The famous "Wally Tantrum" begins!

Mom Shelby feels totally humiliated.

She looks with disbelief as her son rages and the customers watch, waiting for her response.

If you believe Mom Shelby should ...

*... give Wally an appropriate whack and usher him
out of the store,* .... **Turn to Scene 33**

*... say, "You've lost your chance to decide," then pick Wally up
and carry him from the store,* .... **Turn to Scene 34**

With a vengeance Mom Shelby reaches down and gives Wally a whack. Out of the corner of her eye, she notices what appears to be an approving look on the cashier's face.

Mom reaches for Wally's arm to pull him from the store.

Unfortunately, Mom Shelby doesn't notice that Wally is gripping the rickety shelves.

As Mom Shelby yanks Wally away, she hears a gasp come from the cashier. Down fall three shelves of candy! Wally is almost buried beneath candy bars, chewing gum and cough drops.

Mom Shelby watches in horror. The cashier is no longer smiling.

Second Chance! Turn to Scene 32

But first, see **Bribery** (page 194) and the **Bribery Case Study: Dressing for Snacks** in the *A–Z Parenting Guide* (page 194).

SCENE 34

Embarrassed, Mom Shelby picks Wally off the floor and lumbers toward the exit. Wally kicks and screams, trying to escape from her arms. But Mom Shelby is determined.

"You've lost your chance this time," she explains. Despite her anger, Mom Shelby bites her tongue and resists hurling a verbal assault at Wally.

Mom Shelby looks straight ahead as she exits the store. She imagines that the cashier believes that she's a total ogre, and she prays that none of the customers recognize her.

Once in the car, relief begins to push aside Mom Shelby's anxiety and rage. She doesn't even mind Wally's pouting or anger.

As Mom Shelby drives along, she begins to feel pleased: *Finally, I stood up to the monstrous side of Wally. It's about time!*

Wally looks as if he would love to stomp on someone's flower garden. He glances toward Mom Shelby and is stunned by what he sees: Mom Shelby smiling, appearing self-confident.

Dropping off Wally at school, Mom Shelby reminds him: "I won't be home when you return from school. But Dad will be there."

Wally slams the door and walks toward his class.

Mom Shelby drives away, as pleased as a prisoner just paroled.

Turn to Scene 45

SCENE 35

As Mom Shelby dresses, she makes sure not to put on her belt before Wally finishes dressing. Wally loves friendly competition, and Mom Shelby knows he's racing to finish first.

Before Mom Shelby expects him to finish, Wally runs into the room, "I won. I'm dressed!"

Mom Shelby looks at him with admiration, as much for her own ingenuity as for his speed. "You really are quick, Wally."

But Mom Shelby's happiness doesn't last long.

"Mom, I don't want to go to school today," asserts Wally.

"Why not?" asks his Mom.

"My teacher hates me, and I never have time to do things I want to do. It's just not fair!" Wally replies in a grown-up voice.

If you believe Mom Shelby should say ...

> ... *"I'm sorry you feel that way. But lots of things in life aren't fair.*
> *People can't do everything they want. Now let's go,"* .... **Turn to Scene 36**

> ... *"Tell me why you believe your teacher doesn't like you,"* ...... **Turn to Scene 37**

SCENE 36

Mom Shelby has given the "Life's Not Fair" and "No One Gets To Do Everything" speech so many times that she barely bothers to look at Wally as she completes her soliloquy.

Her lack of eye contact doesn't really matter though, because Wally isn't listening anyway.

Instead, he grabs his favorite bear and hangs on to it while Mom Shelby completes her monologue.

When she finishes, Mom Shelby rushes to the car with Wally following, still clutching his bear.

Mom Shelby is worried because Wally is silent on the short trip to his preschool. He just sits, holding his bear and gazing out the window. Wally is rarely quiet unless something is wrong.

Mom Shelby doesn't feel good about leaving Wally while he's looking so disheartened, but *What can I do?* she wonders.

"Remember, Dad will be home when you return from school. I'll be back shortly after that," Mom Shelby encourages.

Wally looks blankly at Mom Shelby, then nods and opens the car door. As he leaves, he manages a mechanical, "Good-bye, I love you."

"I love you, too," assures Mom Shelby. For a moment, she wishes she could scoop Wally into her arms and stay with him the entire morning. But duty calls. And off she rushes toward school.

Turn to Scene 45

SCENE 37

Mom Shelby sits down on the bed beside Wally and asks, "Why do you believe that your teacher doesn't like you?"

"She never lets me do what I want to do," explains Wally.

"And what do you want to do, Wally?" inquires Mom Shelby.

"I just want some time to play by myself. Sometimes I want to draw or play with my figures. Different things. I hate to do what the teacher tells me to do all day long," Wally declares.

If you believe Mom Shelby should say ...

... *"I'm in a terrible rush, but before I go to school today, I will talk to your teacher about giving you more free time,"* .... **Turn to Scene 38**

... *"Wally, I understand that you often don't have free time to play. I promise I'll make a special time tonight for you to do whatever you want,"* .... **Turn to Scene 44**

SCENE 38

Mom Shelby rushes with Wally to his preschool. On the way she feels like kicking herself for promising to talk to Wally's teacher. *Why can Wally charm or bully me into doing anything?* she wonders.

I'm in such a rush! But I guess it won't take but a second, Mom Shelby considers.

Arriving at the school, Mom Shelby and Wally jump out and hurry inside.

"Where is your teacher, Wally?" inquires Mom Shelby.

No sooner does Mom Shelby ask than she sees his teacher talking with obvious concern to another parent. Worse, a line of parents circle the teacher like planes approaching a fogged-in airport.

"Wally, I can't talk to her now. I have to be at school on time," explains Mom Shelby.

"But you promised!" replies Wally, ready to burst into tears.

If you believe Mom Shelby should ...

... *keep her promise and talk with Wally's teacher,* .... **Turn to Scene 39**

... *promise Wally to talk to his teacher later so that she can arrive on time,* .... **Turn to Scene 40**

SCENE 39

Mom Shelby reaffirms her promise to Wally. But minutes seem to pass as slowly as calendar time. Looking at her watch every few seconds, Mom Shelby realizes that she will be late.

She feels a mixture of humiliation, sadness and rage swelling within. *How did she get herself into this situation? Couldn't this parent-teacher conversation wait?*

Mom Shelby realizes that her principal will be irate. Desperate, she starts to interrupt Wally's teacher to steal a moment of time with her. But before she can act, the director of the preschool runs toward Wally's teacher.

After a moment, the director addresses the class, "Students, your teacher has an emergency phone call. I will stay with you for a few minutes until she returns."

Already late, Mom Shelby's chest constricts as Wally tightens the grip on her hand to prevent her from leaving. Mom Shelby knows that whatever she does next will be wrong.

Second Chance! Turn to Scene 38

But first, see **Respect for Self and Others** (page 242)
and **Respect Case Study 1:**
Late for Wally's Sake in the *A–Z Parenting Guide* (page 242).

Mom Shelby kneels down and speaks quietly to Wally: "I will call your teacher tonight and talk with her. I must go now or my students will miss me. Don't worry, we will work things out."

"But you promised you'd talk to her now!" pleads Wally.

"I know honey, but I'll just have to wait until tonight," assures Mom Shelby, kneeling next to Wally.

Although not sure if she had ever felt worse when she left Wally at preschool, Mom Shelby prepares to depart. Wally's body is heaving up and down, as children's do when they don't want to cry but cannot stop.

Mom Shelby kisses Wally's head, then leaves.

In the car, Mom Shelby worries about how Wally will feel during the long day. She's not happy to leave him, but she's positive that she is doing the right thing. She only wishes she could see him before nightfall. At least Dad Shelby will be home early today. Maybe he'll be able to help.

Turn to Scene 45

SCENE 41

Wally's temper tantrum hits high gear, and then he notices that Mom Shelby is no longer in the room.

He continues yelling for a while, but Mom Shelby doesn't return.

Angry, Wally decides to put on his wet shoes. "I'll show Mom. She'll never let me wear these wet shoes. I'll force her to help me. Anything is better than wearing those awful dress shoes," he schemes.

Mom Shelby walks toward the car with Wally close behind. As she starts the engine, Mom Shelby glances toward Wally's feet. "Wet shoes — Wally, how could you?" wonders Mom Shelby.

If you believe Mom Shelby should say ...

... *"If you go change into your dress shoes quickly, we'll buy a snack before school begins,"* . . . . **Turn to Scene 32**

... *"If you believe that Mom should allow Wally to attend preschool in his wet shoes,* . . . . **Turn to Scene 42**

SCENE 42

Mom wants to yell at Wally for being so stubborn, but she resists the temptation.

Wally is constantly testing me. He always assumes I'm going to do what he wants me to. This morning I'm going to let him wear his wet shoes. Maybe that will be the most important lesson I can teach him — and myself, reasons Mom Shelby.

Of course, reason and emotions are two different things. As a mother, Mom Shelby feels terrible thinking about how miserable Wally might become. Also, she worries about what Wally's teacher might think of her for allowing a preschooler to wear wet shoes.

Nevertheless, Mom Shelby decides the lesson will be worth any embarrassment she feels. As they arrive at the preschool, it's obvious that Wally cannot believe that Mom Shelby is going to allow him to attend school wearing wet shoes.

"But Mom, do you want me to catch a cold?" inquires a dumbfounded Wally. "Of course not," replies Mom Shelby. "But I want to respect your decision."

Bewildered, Wally leaves the car. Mom Shelby drives away. As she looks in the rear view mirror, she sees Wally remove his shoes. Somewhat comforted, Mom Shelby realizes that the teacher is about to hear another one of Wally's adventure tales. "Thank heaven," reflects Mom, "I can go to work and relax. Work is my play."

Turn to Scene 45

"**O.K.,** Wally," bargains Mom Shelby, "I'll help you with your pants and shirt. You be in charge of finding your socks and shoes and putting them on."

Wally seems less than happy with the arrangement. But at least he can finish dressing by himself.

Mom tries to dress the fidgety Wally. He helps as little as possible. She's annoyed, but knows better than to ignite his temper now.

Finally, the job completed, Mom Shelby reminds Wally, "Remember that we're in a rush. Put on your shoes quickly and come out to the car."

Wally searches for a pair of socks. He doesn't really like any of his choices, but he puts on a pair of sports socks, anyway. Then he begins to search for his shoes. After looking under everything in his room, he finally glances toward the window sill. There are his shoes!

Wally wanders over to the window before he remembers why he left them in the window. "Oh, no!" exclaims Wally. "My shoes got soaked when I was spraying Wendy with the water hose yesterday."

Turn to Scene 26

SCENE 44

"Tonight after supper you can play for 30 minutes. That's a long time, and no one will bother you," promises Mom Shelby.

"But I want to play now," replies Wally.

"I understand," explains Mom Shelby. "But you'll just have to wait. We really need to move quickly now, Wally. I appreciate how well you've dressed by yourself. But you forgot your shoes. Put them on and we'll be ready to leave."

Wally nods his head and begins to look for his shoes. Mom Shelby hurries out of the room to prepare to leave.

Turn to Scene 88

SCENE 45

Dad Shelby's work day ends, and he's exhausted. How wonderful it is to come home, he thinks.

Shortly after Dad Shelby arrives, the children come home from school and are immediately captured by the "Brainless," Mom Shelby's pet word for their television. For an instant he considers, *Maybe I should go outside and play basketball with them.*

Wrong! concludes Dad Shelby. *They're quiet for once, and I want to read the newspaper and unwind.*

No sooner does Dad Shelby sit down to read the paper than Mom Shelby returns home from work.

"I'll put supper on the stove if you'll watch the kids," bargains Mom Shelby.

"Sure. I'll be glad to help," replies Dad Shelby. *What a deal!* Dad Shelby reflects. *I haven't heard a word from them for ten minutes.*

As if Dad Shelby's thoughts could magically invoke disaster, a bloodcurdling scream from Wally pierces the quiet. Wendy runs to summon the parental cavalry for help: "William's killing Wally!"

Immediately, Dad Shelby charges into the crime scene. There, he finds William — red-faced and angry — standing over the fallen Wally. Soaked by fresh tears, Wally looks helplessly at Dad Shelby and pleads, "He hit me for no reason."

William retorts, "That's not true, Wally started it . . . ."

If you believe Dad Shelby should ...

... *discipline William, who is older and should know better, no matter what happened,* .... **Go on to Scene 46**

... *call Mom Shelby in to help decide what to do,* .... **Turn to Scene 48**

... *send all three children, including the two fighters and the stool pigeon, to their rooms to cool off,* .... **Turn to Scene 47**

SCENE 46

Dad Shelby yells at William, "I don't want to hear it; you're older; you should know better." He delivers a smack to William's backside, then orders him to his room. William yells over his shoulder, "I hate you! Everyone blames me for everything."

As William screams, a little smile slips over Wally's face. Unfortunately for Wally, the smirk doesn't escape Dad Shelby's attention. A sickening feeling overtakes Dad Shelby. "Okay, Wally, what did you do?"

"It wasn't my fault," protests Wally. "How did I know his stupid airplane couldn't fly?" In one corner, the wreckage of William's model airplane litters the floor.

If you believe Dad Shelby should ...

... *give Wally a swat and send him to his room,* .... **Turn to Scene 49**

... *talk to William to discuss what really happened,* .... **Turn to Scene 50**

... *say, You should know better, anyway. Wally, from now on leave your brother's things alone,"* .... **Turn to Scene 51**

SCENE 47

"All three of you go to your rooms. This fighting must end. Think about your part in the fight," demands Dad Shelby.

Wendy is outraged to be sent to her room. "I'm innocent! Nobody ever listens to me," she protests. A low wail stirs from Wendy's room. Soon it swells into a cry that soars up and down as tumultuously as Old Faithful.

Mom Shelby quietly walks to the door and listens. Wendy moans, half to herself and half to a cruel world, "Nobody loves me. William and Wally get away with murder. Everyone picks on me. It's not fair."

If you believe Mom Shelby should ...

... *Open the door and give Wendy a hug and reassurance,* ...... **Turn to Scene 72**

... *Walk away and talk to Wendy at some later time,* .... **Turn to Scene 67**

Dad calls Mom Shelby.

"What's going on in here? Can't I have two minutes to myself without my family falling apart?" bellows an annoyed Mom Shelby.

Dad Shelby explains, "I came in after William belted Wally. William should know better; I've told him so many times . . . ."

"Well, why did you call me?" interrupts Mom Shelby impatiently. "What am I supposed to do about it?"

Mom and Dad Shelby glare at each other.

Uncomfortable, Wendy intervenes, "I don't think Wally is hurt that badly."

If you believe the Shelbys should say ...

... *"Children, solve this problem yourselves, your parents need to talk",* .... **Turn to Scene 52**

... *"Wendy, stay out of this. William, apologize to Wally this minute, and I don't want you two ever fighting in this house again,"* ... **Turn to Scene 61**

SCENE 49

Properly swatted, Wally screams every step of the way back to his room: "It wasn't my fault. It wasn't my fault!"

Slamming the door as hard as he can, Wally dives onto his bed, sobbing.

After five minutes of Wally's tantrums, an eerie silence fills the house. Suddenly, a crashing sound comes from Wally's room. Dad Shelby doesn't need long to figure out that Wally has just overturned his bookshelf in protest.

Rage swells through the veins in Dad Shelby's neck.

If you believe Dad Shelby should ...

... count to ten before acting, ... **Turn to Scene 82**

... enter Wally's room and confront the miscreant's misdeed directly and immediately, ... **Turn to Scene 81**

SCENE 50

Dad Shelby asks William to return to the living room to discuss the crime. William struggles to tell his side of the story, but his chest heaves with indignation.

As William takes a deep breath to try to control his emotions, Wally takes the opportunity to interrupt: "William's always picking on me. He's a bully."

Dad Shelby refuses to be baited. "Wally, be quiet and let William tell his side of the story."

Feeling Dad Shelby's support, William takes heart: "I told Wally to leave my things alone. He's always messing in my stuff. I tried to grab the plane out of his hands, but he threw it as hard as he could against the wall."

"That's not true!" howls Wally.

"What's not true?" asks Dad Shelby.

"That's not as hard as I can throw it," responds Wally indignantly.

The truth now being out, what should Dad Shelby do?

If you believe that he should:

... *give Wally the swat on the rear that he mistakenly gave to William,* ....**Turn to Scene 86**

... *apologize to William for accusing him wrongly and talk privately with Wally about replacing the plane,* ....**Turn to Scene 87**

SCENE 51

"**F**rom now on leave your brother's things alone," Dad Shelby reprimands Wally.

"I will," Wally promises with a tone of relief. Walking back to his room, Wally discovers Wendy's unguarded doll carriage. After trying without success to stuff Wizard the cat into the buggy, Wally grows frustrated. Quickly rolling the carriage to the top of the stairs, he shoves it over the edge.

End over end the buggy bounds. On cue, Wendy runs to the top of the stairs to investigate. Seeing her treasure crumpled at the bottom of the steps, Wendy screams for Mom Shelby's assistance using a tone saved for occasions when she's undeniably in the right.

Mom Shelby understands that Wendy has suffered a wrong that requires instant justice. Inspecting the accident scene, Mom needs only a glance to piece together the recent chain of events.

If you believe Mom Shelby should ...

... *tell Wally to retrieve the carriage and fix it,* ....**Turn to Scene 78**

... *tell Wendy to calm down and then explain that Wally was frustrated and didn't mean to damage her buggy,* ....**Turn to Scene 80**

SCENE 52

Mom Shelby grabs Dad Shelby by the sleeve and pulls him into their bedroom. Normally, Dad Shelby would be ecstatic to be pulled in that direction, but at this moment he realizes that he's about to enter a battle that no one can win.

"I'm sick and tired of your calling me when the children misbehave. When are you going to start acting like a father?" interrogates Mom Shelby.

Until his role as a father was questioned, Dad Shelby planned to endure Mom Shelby's tongue-lashing without so much as a whimper. But now his wife has ventured too far.

Dad Shelby asserts, "I already act like a father. When there's trouble with one of our children, I try to communicate with you."

"That's not communication," retorts Mom Shelby, "that's cowardice. You want the children to like you and you want me to be the bad guy."

"Well, not all the time," replies Dad Shelby without premeditation. Then, realizing his confession, he takes the offensive. "Things used to be better before you decided to go back to work . . . ."

Dad Shelby knowingly crossed into forbidden territory. The couple frequently disagree, but the Shelbys share an unwritten rule that prohibits bringing up raw, painful topics.

A woman wronged, Mom Shelby unleashes a tirade.

Turn to Scene 53

SCENE 53

The Shelby children flock outside of their parents' bedroom, nervously eavesdropping, but sensing they shouldn't. As their parents' voices become angry, the Shelby children are deathly silent. William mechanically throws a ball up and down. Wally, seemingly less concerned, draws in his coloring book. Wendy creeps closer to her parents' door.

As the discussion becomes more heated, Wendy feels increasingly desperate. Suddenly she throws open the door to her parents' retreat and blurts out: "Isn't it about time for supper?"

Shock covers the faces of the parents. The proverbial calm before the storm fills the room.

If you believe that ...

... Mom Shelby should respond, "Wendy, our disagreement does not concern you. Please wait outside until we finish talking," . . . . . **Turn to Scene 54**

... Dad should forcefully let Wendy know that she should never interrupt, ... **Turn to Scene 60**

SCENE 54

Mom Shelby gently places her hand on Wendy's shoulder and explains, "Sometimes parents disagree and we lose our tempers. But Dad and I love each other and we love all of you. This disagreement has nothing to do with any of you. Why don't all of you run outside and play for a few minutes?"

Wendy obviously feels relieved. Before leaving the room, she gives Mom a hug and looks sheepishly at Dad, who may have different ideas. Satisfied, Wendy strolls out of the bedroom.

"Let's go," Wendy yells to her brothers as she walks out of the house. She knows they'll follow her. Not only do they regard her as a hero for her entry into potentially hostile territory, but also they want to hear her espionage report first hand.

As they hear their children leave the house, Mom and Dad Shelby look at each other with embarrassment and regret.

"I'm sorry," Dad Shelby admits. "I had such a rough day at the office."

Recognizing how weak his excuse is, Mom Shelby, nevertheless, allows her husband to save face. After all, in a crisis someone must act like an adult.

"Still," reflects Mom Shelby, "we haven't really solved anything."

Go on to Scene 55

SCENE 55

Wendy's prestigious position doesn't last long. In moments, the Shelby children discover a new challenge.

"I bet neither of you can climb the Carlsons' fence and run across their yard!" challenges William.

"Their dog might bite me," declares a terrified Wally.

"No he won't. He's chained up so he won't dig in their flower garden," notes William peevishly.

Wendy reverses the challenge, "It was your idea, why don't you do it? Scared?"

Wendy always knows the screws to turn and William responds as predictably as usual: "I'm not scared of anything. Watch this!"

With that William scales the chain link fence and drops to the other side. The Carlsons' dog, Liberty, barks hysterically at the intruder. William looks around, but the Carlsons don't seem to be anywhere nearby.

William runs to the opposite side of the Carlsons' yard. The dog chases William furiously. Suddenly Liberty's chain straightens and he's snapped into the air, then lands with a thud on the ground.

William can't stand the temptation. Carefully estimating the length of Liberty's chain, William runs in a circle just outside of the dog's grasp. Soon Liberty's chain becomes hopelessly tangled around the Carlson's prized herd of ceramic deer.

Enjoying his crime too much, William neglects to watch out for the Carlsons. When the youngster finally looks, he sees Mr. Carlson staring in horror out of the kitchen window.

William scampers across the yard, back toward the chain link fence. There is no sign of Wendy and Wally, who long ago knew that William was headed for disaster.

"What do you think you're doing, you little jerk!" yells an enraged Mr. Carlson.

Mr. Carlson runs toward William, but he's too late. William climbs the fence and drops to the safer side. Never looking back, the villain flees into the Shelby sanctuary.

After freeing Liberty from the herd of deer, Mr. Carlson enters his home and phones Dad Shelby. In the meantime, all three Shelby children steal into their rooms and begin playing as innocently as monks.

Dad Shelby answers the phone and hears Mr. Carlson's furious voice: "Shelby, your ruthless children have been at it again. When are you going to teach them to behave! They trespassed into my yard and terrorized Liberty. What are you going to do to punish your hoodlums?"

If you believe that Dad Shelby should respond ...

... "I'm sorry for what my children did. I will handle the situation immediately," .... **Turn to Scene 56**

... "Kids will be kids, Mr. Carlson. But in some ways you're being more childish than they were," .... **Turn to Scene 59**

SCENE 56

"**C**hildren!" yells Mr. Shelby after impatiently slamming the receiver back on the hook. "Come here this instant."

In walk the Shelby kids, an angelic glow shining from each face.

Dad Shelby begins, "Mr. Carlson said that you trespassed on his land and you threatened Liberty. What do you have to say about that?"

Wendy lies first: "We were just playing ball. I accidentally threw the ball over the fence and William climbed over to get it. We didn't want to bother you and Mom."

Understanding Wendy's drift, William adds, "When I got over the fence, Liberty attacked me. I was running from him when Mr. Carlson began to call me names."

"Mr. Carlson called him a jerk," Wally added. At his young age, Wally has not cultivated the art of deception. In fact, he's rather certain that Wendy's and William's version is probably the truth. After repeating the story several times, Wendy and William will soon forget the truth as well.

If you believe Dad Shelby should ...

... *ground the kids for the day,* .... **Turn to Scene 57**

... *ask them to apologize to Mr. Carlson,* .... **Turn to Scene 58**

SCENE 57

"I know that you don't believe you did anything wrong. But it's wrong to go into the Carlsons' yard without their permission — no matter what the reason. Now I want each of you to stay in your room until supper time," declares Dad Shelby in a firm but kind voice.

"That's not fair. It was Mr. Carlson's fault," challenges an innocent Wally.

"Come on, Wally," interrupts William. "Let's go to our rooms. Forget Mr. Carlson." William knows that it's not in his best interest to keep this conversation alive.

Pulling Wally by the sleeve, William leaves the room.

Dad Shelby knows that Mr. Carlson's version is probably true, but what else could he have done? He backed his children, and in a way he supported Mr. Carlson.

Dad Shelby returns to his reading chair, but he can't concentrate. He feels enraged, but at whom?

At least, he hopes, dinner time may go more smoothly.

Turn to Scene 96

SCENE 58

"Children," begins Dad Shelby, "to go into the Carlsons' yard without their permission was wrong. I want you to call Mr. Carlson and apologize. You three decide who should call. I'll check on things later."

After his proclamation, Dad Shelby leaves the room. Shocked by this turn of events, William and Wendy stare at each other.

"Don't look at *me*, William," exclaims Wendy. "It was *your* great idea. Wally and I didn't trespass."

"But what should I say?" inquires William, resigned that he cannot win a debate with Wendy on many topics, especially this one.

"Just tell him you're sorry and you won't do it again. That usually works," suggests Wendy.

William looks forlorn. Wendy sees her opportunity.

"What's wrong William? Scared?" she challenges contemptuously.

"Of course not," asserts William.

He knows he's being manipulated by Wendy, but he's too anxious to figure out exactly how she's pulling his strings.

Slowly, he walks to the phone.

"I don't know the number," he sighs with relief.

But there stands Wendy, number in hand.

William dials the number, and Mr. Carlson answers the phone.

"Mr. Carlson, I just want to say I'm sorry I went into your yard, and I won't ever do it again," declares William in his most repentant voice.

"William, I appreciate your calling," replies a shocked Mr. Carlson. "It takes quite a person to admit a mistake. Someday I want you to come over and make friends with Liberty. You hurt his feelings today."

"I'm sorry, sir. It won't happen again, and I'd like to play with Liberty someday," replies William as sincerely as possible. The young criminal doesn't know whether to feel condemned or excited at the prospect of playing with Liberty — a dog he now blames for most of his troubles.

"O.K., son. We'll consider this event finished. Thanks for calling. Good-bye," says Mr. Carlson in the nicest voice William has ever heard him use.

William hangs up the phone, feeling exuberant. Having confronted his adversary, he feels like a real adult. Confidently and condescendingly, he strolls past Wendy.

"I'll be in my room if you wish to talk with me," he says in a superior voice to no one in particular. "Call me when dinner is ready."

"What an idiot," comments Wendy, vainly trying to cut William back to size.

Turn to Scene 96

54

"Childish!" shouts Mr. Carlson. "Look who's being childish! Your children trespassed on my property and teased Liberty and you're yelling at me?"

Despite not feeling entirely on solid ground, Dad Shelby accepts the challenge and escalates: "Mr. Carlson, if you and your wife weren't such hostile neighbors, looking for every little thing to complain about, these incidents wouldn't happen."

"Oh, now it's my fault your lousy kids trespassed on my property!" exclaims Mr. Carlson.

Clinging to any straw he can, Dad Shelby yells, "Don't call my kids 'lousy'! Besides, my children didn't do any harm."

"Maybe we should let the police decide whether or not trespassing and humiliating Liberty are crimes," righteously proclaims Mr. Carlson.

"Go ahead. Call the police. See if I care," challenges a defeated Dad Shelby before slamming the receiver down.

Mr. Carlson slowly dials the police station. No longer is his gripe with the Shelby kids; Dad Shelby simply went too far this time.

"Hello, police. I need help," Mr. Carlson begins.

Second Chance! Turn to Scene 55
But first, see **Permissiveness** (page 232) and **Permissiveness Case Study 2: Barking up the Wrong Tree** in the *A–Z Parenting Guide* (page 234).

"**W**endy, get your rear end out of this room this instant. If I want to hear words come out of your mouth, I'll let you know," callously asserts Dad Shelby.

"Don't you talk to Wendy in that tone," Mom Shelby responds protectively.

"She's my daughter and I'll talk to her any way I want to," counters Dad Shelby.

"Not as long as I'm alive," escalates Mom Shelby.

Wendy backs away from Dad Shelby. Instinctively, he reaches to grab her arm. Too quick for him, Mom Shelby pulls Wendy away.

Firmly holding her daughter, Mom Shelby warns, "Don't you ever touch my child in anger."

Dad Shelby stands stunned. How was a quiet moment in his reading chair transformed into a world class struggle in two minutes?

Humiliated, Dad Shelby says nothing, walks out of the room and leaves the Shelby home. "Maybe a drink will help me understand what just happened," Dad Shelby reflects sadly.

Second Chance! Turn to Scene 53

But first, see **Marriage** (page 222) and **Marriage Case Study 1: Parental Split** in the *A–Z Parenting Guide* (page 223).

SCENE 61

Wendy and William look with amazement at Mom Shelby. It's not like her to make hasty judgments. Neither child follows through on Mom Shelby's demands.

But their behavior isn't noticed. Clearly, Mom Shelby's attention is focused on Dad Shelby.

"Come with me. We need to talk!" Mom Shelby commands her husband.

Already feeling betrayed by his wife, Dad Shelby follows Mom Shelby into the bedroom. He's not sure where the discussion will lead, but after being embarrassed before his children, he's determined to stand up for himself.

"Why is it that every time there's a problem with the children you call me? You make me so angry!" begins Mom Shelby.

"If you owned half a brain, you wouldn't make me look incompetent in front of the children, even if you are mad," sharply counters Dad Shelby.

Mom Shelby knows that she can either drop this fight or escalate it, but she's far too annoyed to let go.

"Well, let's just put all our cards on the table," suggests Mom Shelby with the certainty of someone playing with a loaded deck.

Dad Shelby isn't intimidated. Apparently, he has a few aces to play as well.

Turn to Scene 62

SCENE 62

As Mom and Dad Shelby's voices grow angrier, their children become increasingly anxious. The only sound to be heard besides the Shelby parents arguing is Wally as he plays aggressively with his toy figures:

"I'll bash your brains out," Wally makes the bad guy say. "But here comes Super Charger to the rescue! The hero pounds the bad guy and lets all the prisoners go."

If only real life could be so simple!

Over Wally's voice, Mom and Dad can occasionally be heard. William walks toward their door to listen.

What he overhears alarms him: Dad Shelby is in a rage.

"You always take the side of the children over me, and I'm sick of it. Some day you're going to regret it!" says Dad Shelby in a threatening tone.

William doesn't understand what is happening, but is frightened by Dad Shelby's tone of voice. William throws open the bedroom door and gallantly declares, "Leave my mother alone!"

The Shelby parents are shocked. In the quiet moment that follows, the tension mounts like a roller coaster reaching the peak of its incline. Finally, Dad Shelby must respond to William's intrusion . . . .

If you believe that Dad Shelby should ...

> *... let William know once and for all not to intervene*
> *in the Shelbys' marital spats,* .... **Turn to Scene 63**

> *... be patient and assure William that everything will be fine,* ... **Turn to Scene 64**

58

"**Y**oung man, you've poked your head into a place it doesn't belong. Leave this room *now,*" demands Dad Shelby in his most authoritarian style.

Normally William would retreat instantly. But one can never tell where mixed loyalties and a call to gallantry might lead a child.

The sound of William's own defiant voice breaking the silence surprises the youngster as much as it surprises his parents: "I'm not leaving."

No sooner do the words leave William's mouth than Dad Shelby's open hand sails toward its target. Landing squarely on William's cheek, the slap causes the youngster to stumble back.

Looking up, William sees Mom Shelby in tears. Dad's eyes are still filled with anger. William knows that the skirmish is over, and that he severely underestimated Dad Shelby's reaction.

The Shelbys enter one of those awful crossroads: The next move anyone makes will probably be a wrong one.

Second Chance! Turn to Scene 62

But first, see **Marriage** (page 222) and **Marriage Case Study 2: William Enters the Lion's Den** in the *A–Z Parenting Guide* (page 224).

Dad Shelby seems stunned by William's intrusion.

Finally, he gathers his wits and responds, "William, I'm pleased to see your support for your mother. I'm sorry if our disagreement disturbed you. Even adults who love one another lose their tempers occasionally. As you can see, everything is fine. Just give us an opportunity to talk things over for a few minutes."

William looks skeptically toward Mom Shelby. She nods her assent, and William reluctantly leaves the room.

Not entirely trusting the situation, William stays close by the door to monitor the tone of the conversation.

Although the Shelby parents muffle their discussion, it obviously is becoming overheated once more.

William knows he can't burst into the room again to stop their fight. But what can he do?

Discouraged, he goes down to the basement.

In the midst of their skirmish, Mom Shelby begins to sniff the air. Her look of concern sets off an alarm within Dad Shelby. He too smells the air.

"Smoke!" they both declare.

Running toward the basement, the Shelby parents yell *"Fire! Fire!"* to alert anyone within hearing distance.

As the Shelby adults enter the basement, they see smoke coming from under the workroom door.

After they throw open the door, the Shelbys eye William standing in the corner. Two feet away from him, smoke still billows from a pile of old rags used to clean the Shelby work tools. But the fire is now out.

William has a confused and troubled look about him. Obviously, the youngster is the culprit. After disposing of the smoking materials, Dad Shelby turns toward his sheepish son.

If you believe that Dad Shelby should ...

... tell William that he will help him find a good counselor,...... **Turn to Scene 65**

... ask William why he set the fire, ... **Turn to Scene 66**

SCENE 65

"William, I've had it with you. I just cannot take it any more. They have a word for this — pyromania!" shouts Dad in an accusatory voice.

Mom Shelby adds, "William, I'm very concerned that you would do something as dangerous as this. You could have hurt or even killed yourself — and the rest of us."

Dad Shelby's glance meets Mom Shelby's. Her demeanor suggests that she will back whatever suggestion Dad Shelby is about to make.

"William, I love you too much to let you behave like this. I think it's about time that you talk to a professional about some of the things bothering you. I'll call a counselor first thing in the morning," asserts Dad Shelby.

"But *you two* are my problem," interjects William.

"Save it for the counselor, son," suggests Dad Shelby. "I'm sure you have things you need to talk about that I just wouldn't understand."

"But *I* don't need a counselor. *You* do!" attacks William.

"That will be quite enough from you, young man," Mom Shelby intervenes. "Your father is only doing what's best for you."

Seeing that his parents agree upon his sentence, William slumps his shoulders and slowly walks toward his bedroom.

Once there, he throws himself onto his bed and begins a vengeful daydream: "I wish both of them were on a train and the bridge ahead collapsed and . . . ."

Second Chance! Turn to Scene 64

But first, see **Marriage** (page 222) and **Marriage Case Study 3:**
Sacrificial Flame in the *A–Z Parenting Guide* (page 225).

SCENE 66

Stunned, Dad Shelby takes a moment to pull together his thoughts. *This is truly unlike William*, he reflects.

After considering various possibilities, Dad Shelby confesses, "I'm at a loss for words, William. Why did you set this fire? You knew you would be caught."

William looks sheepishly at the floor. "I don't know," the felon claims.

But something in William's voice leads Mom Shelby to venture a guess. "William, does this fire have something to do with Dad Shelby and me?"

Tears spill down William's face. He hangs his head and discloses, "I can't stand it when the two of you fight."

"And you thought the fire would stop us," Mom Shelby offers.

"I don't know what I thought. I just had to do something. I'm sorry. The fire was stupid," confesses William.

"It sure was," declares Dad Shelby in a gruff but understanding way. Clearly, Dad Shelby feels uncomfortable seeing emotions shared so openly. But his tolerant tone displays his receptivity, even if he does feel self-conscious.

"William, we understand," Mom Shelby says softly. "Clean up this mess and finish your homework before supper."

Turn to Scene 96

Mom Shelby walks away from Wendy's room. *Wendy has become a terrible tattletale,* reflects Mom Shelby. *She creates as many problems by meddling into William and Wally's business as the boys' fights do. Some times I believe she eggs on their disagreements just to look angelic herself.*

With this concluding thought Mom Shelby convinces herself that giving each child the same consequence was a good idea. Feeling better, she returns to her supper preparations.

After a few tearful eruptions, Wendy realizes no one is likely to come to her aid. She is more than annoyed at being treated like the common criminal she believes her siblings to be. But worse than aggravated, she has also become bored.

An idea strikes Wendy. Immediately, she knocks three times on the wall that separates her room from William's. Responding to the signal, William knocks three times.

Anxious to be co-conspirators rather than adversaries, William and Wendy meet in the hallway.

Turn to Scene 68

SCENE 68

"**W**hat's up?" William inquires eagerly.

"Let's sneak to the grocery store and buy some candy," urges Wendy.

"Yeah, that's a great idea! Should we take Wally along?" inquires William.

"Sure," schemes Wendy. "In case we're caught he'll be good protection. Mom and Dad Shelby never punish Wally very much. But let's make him promise to be absolutely quiet."

After a few moments Wally and William appear at the door of Wendy's room.

"Come on in," she says quietly. "We'll sneak out of my window."

"Why don't we just go out the front door?" questions the ever-logical William.

"Because that's no fun!" replies Wendy with enough indignation to show William how little he knows about adventure.

In the grocery store, Wendy and William storm the aisles like looters. After selecting several candy bars, they search for Wally. After locating their prodigal brother, William and Wendy pull him toward the checkout counter.

"What did you find, Wally?" William asks.

"Nothing. I don't want anything," Wally asserts with a strange tone in his voice.

Out of the store, the three walk toward home. Suddenly a clerk bursts from the store and charges toward them. As he reaches the startled children, the clerk shouts at Wally, "What do you have in your pockets, young man?"

"Nothing," maintains Wally.

"Then empty your pockets, please!" requests the clerk.

In seconds, four crumpled candy bars come out of Wally's pockets and he offers a weak explanation: "I didn't have any money."

At that precise moment, the Shelby children look up to see Dad Shelby down the block watching the entire scenario.

If you believe that Dad Shelby should ...

... keep watching and allow the children to handle the problem themselves, ... **Turn to Scene 69**

... intervene to make sure justice is done, ... **Turn to Scene 188**

SCENE 69

Dad Shelby takes a step backward. *Obviously, he's not going to become involved,* figures Wendy.

"Sir," she addresses the clerk. "I have enough money to pay for the candy. Wally's too young to know what he was doing. I'll pay."

The clerk seems pleased to discover a way out of the situation: "That's fine. Let's return to the store and I'll ring up the merchandise. But young man," he chastises Wally, "what you did was terribly wrong."

Wally is frightened beyond tears. This is his first brush with the law outside of his home. Even William and Wendy feel slightly sympathetic toward him. Nevertheless, their feelings won't prevent them from seeking revenge for this public humiliation.

After coming out of the store, the Shelby children realize that Dad Shelby will try them a second time. They now join him for what seems like an interminably long walk home. Not saying a word, Dad Shelby's silence seems worse than prison.

Once home, the Shelby children know that Dad will finally deliver his sentence.

If you believe that Dad Shelby should ...

> ... surprise them and ask, "What do you think I should do
> with you?" .... **Turn to Scene 71**

> ... take their allowances away for one month to punish them
> for sneaking out to go to the store, ... **Turn to Scene 70**

SCENE 70

"**Y**ou three have shown me that you cannot be trusted and that you are not responsible with money," Dad Shelby observes. "For that reason I'm taking away your allowances for the entire month. I'm very disappointed. But maybe this time you'll learn about honesty and responsibility."

Even though they weren't involved in the shoplifting, William and Wendy, the ringleaders of the adventure, know better than to protest. Besides, what a relief it is to have Dad Shelby finally end the crisis. The results could have been worse.

"After all," William reflects, "sometimes Dad makes us think of our own consequences. We were lucky."

As the three children go outside, William turns to Wendy and says, "Thanks for paying for the candy. We could have been in *big* trouble. As for you, Wally — what a thief!"

Wally looks as forlorn as Wendy does heroic.

Turn to Scene 55

"What do you believe I should do with you three?" Dad Shelby inquires after returning home. "You sneaked out of your rooms and created a terrible scene at the store."

"Don't do anything," suggests Wally.

"I'm going to do something, Wally. I just want to give you three a chance to decide what's fair," responds Dad Shelby.

"Maybe you could ground us for two months," suggests William, who prefers the most terrible punishment to deliberations of this sort.

"Would it take two months of grounding to give you enough time to think about how dangerous it was for you to sneak off without telling Mom and me?" questions Dad.

"NO! It won't take me that long," offers the quick-witted Wendy.

"Then how long?" questions Dad Shelby.

"Let's say — one week," suggests Wendy.

"Does that sound fair to the rest of you?" asks Dad Shelby. All nod their approval, realizing that Wendy usually forges the best possible deal.

"O.K. We're agreed. The three of you must stay in the house for a week, except to attend school, school events, or any activities that have already been set up," notes an official Dad Shelby.

"Now go to your rooms until supper is ready, please," instructs Dad Shelby.

Turn to Scene 96

SCENE 72

Mom Shelby's heart breaks listening to Wendy cry. Before you can say "softy," Mom Shelby sits beside Wendy and tries in vain to comfort her.

Wendy's sobbing becomes worse and so does Mom Shelby's need to help her.

Wendy complains between gasps, "William and Wally are mean, terrible jerks. They're always getting me into trouble. But I'm the one you and Dad punish. It's not fair."

Mom Shelby automatically defends her children, no matter who attacks them. As if by reflex, she counters, "Wendy, if you didn't tell on them every time they misbehaved, maybe things would be easier for you."

"I don't tell on them *every* time," claims Wendy in her own defense. "You don't know some of the terrible things they've done."

Wendy places herself in the difficult situation of possibly needing to prove that she isn't a tattletale by tattling.

On the other hand, Mom Shelby must either ignore Wendy to display her dislike for tattling or satisfy her curiosity by asking Wendy to name those "terrible things."

If you believe Mom Shelby should ...

> ... *take a deep breath and ask, "What terrible things?"* .... **Turn to Scene 73**

> ... *ignore Wendy's statement and leave,* .... **Turn to Scene 92**

SCENE 73

"Tell me what terrible things your brothers did. I know it can't be too bad," hopes Mom Shelby with a desperate reluctance characteristic of parents and priests at confession.

"They didn't mean to kill the Carlsons' cat," blurts Wendy.

The fury begins in Mom Shelby's toes and rises inch by inch until Wendy is sure that she can see smoke pouring from her nostrils.

Go on to Scene 74

SCENE 74

"William, Wally — come in here, *NOW!"* Mom Shelby orders. Her tone carries a firmness reserved for extraordinary emergencies. In these rare instances, the children run toward Mom Shelby, not even taking enough time to dread what awaits them. They realize that failing to react immediately risks certain doom.

Assembled, the brothers hear the dreaded words: "The Carlsons' cat."

Hatred and terror alternate as William looks back and forth from Wendy to Mom Shelby.

"Don't even look at your sister, William!" directs Mom. "Tell me what happened."

Before William can answer, Wally notes, as if still amazed, "Cats can't breathe under water."

"Under water!" Mom exclaims. "You mean you drowned the Carlsons' cat?"

"Well, sort of," William partially confesses. "We really thought it could get out of the bag. I didn't tie the knot tight. And Dad told us cats were good swimmers and had nine lives and . . . and besides we took it out of the fish pond and buried it by the oak tree."

"I can't believe this. My own children killed the Carlsons' cat," screeches Mom Shelby.

"Not me, I didn't," Wendy corrects.

"No, but you kept it a secret, Wendy. As far as I'm concerned that's like being part of this conspiracy."

By this time Dad Shelby not only has arrived on the scene but also knows the entire story. Anger rarely is more fierce than in a parent who feels humiliated by his children.

The only problem now is which parent will gain the right to discipline the outlaws.

If you agree with ...

... *Mom Shelby, who wants to talk about what the children did and why it was wrong,* ....**Turn to Scene 76**

... *Dad Shelby, who believes the time for talking is over and the time for physical punishment to begin has arrived,* .. **Turn to Scene 75**

SCENE 75

Dad Shelby orders the children to stand in line and broadcasts their sentence: "This spanking is long overdue. William, you're going to get the worst of it, because you were the instigator. Wally, you must learn not to copy William. Wendy, you should have told us. "

As Dad Shelby grabs William by the britches, Mom Shelby intervenes. "Just what do you think you're doing?" she indignantly asks Dad Shelby.

"I'm teaching these children a lesson that's long past due," responds Dad Shelby.

"Not in this house, you're not," Mom Shelby declares.

Dad's anger quickly transfers from the children to Mom Shelby. Trying to stay under control, he stalks off toward the Shelby parents' bedroom and asks Mom Shelby to follow.

The two enter the bedroom and soon their voices grow loud with rage.

Turn to Scene 62

SCENE 76

"How do you think the Carlsons felt when they couldn't find their cat?"Mom Shelby asks.

"I guess they were pretty upset," says William. William is sincere, but also genuinely worried about the possible outcome of this line of questioning.

"Wally," begins Mom Shelby, "how do you think the cat felt — trapped inside the bag and drowning?"

"She wanted to get out," Wally replies, as if he could still see the struggle.

"Mom, I swear I'll never hurt an animal again," declares William. "It was awful. I thought you couldn't kill a cat. Dad always says that they're tougher than lust to stomp out."

"What's a lust?" asks Wally.

"Never mind," Mom continues. "Tell me what you think you three should do now."

Turn to Scene 93

SCENE 77

Finally, the inevitable conclusion confronts William and Wendy. Both are old enough to know that Mom Shelby will settle for nothing less than their facing the Carlsons personally.

William, feeling more responsible for the atrocity, speaks first: "I guess you want me to go to the Carlsons and apologize. Maybe I could offer to do some work around their yard to help make up for it."

Mom Shelby nods approvingly and says, "I think talking to them would require terrific courage, but it won't make up for their cat. However, all three of you need to go together. Don't even think about trying to get out of this, Wendy. William will need your support."

"But what exactly should I say?" asks William.

"We can practice, if that will help," replies Mom Shelby.

After a practice session, the three Shelby children walk slowly to the Carlsons' house. Mom and Dad Shelby stand in the yard close enough to intervene in case anything unexpected arises. Mom Shelby knows the Carlsons well enough to predict that their rage will be softened by the bold presence of the children.

William knocks on the door. Mr. Carlson answers and the confession begins. Obviously upset, Mr. Carlson chastises the children. But the Shelby parents can tell he respects their courage. Future yard work is agreed upon and the children run home, but they will never feel free of the horrible memory of what they did.

Maybe supper time will go more smoothly . . . .

Turn to Scene 96

SCENE 78

"**W**ally Shelby," Mom Shelby uses lasts names to indicate that a coming verdict is non-negotiable, "fetch the doll carriage and fix it to your sister's satisfaction."

Knowing that Mom Shelby's tone is too authoritative to contend with, Wally drags the doll carriage back up the steps. A couple of screws are loose.

"Mom, I can't fix this," fusses Wally.

"I will help you. Fetch the toolbox and we will work on it together," promises Mom Shelby.

Wendy watches over the scene like the foreman of a road crew, obviously free from any obligation to labor. Mom Shelby selects the proper tools but makes certain that Wally does the work.

Afterwards, Wally seems pleased with himself and Wendy feels supported.

"Maybe the three of you should spend some time in your rooms cooling off before supper begins," suggests Mom Shelby.

"Good!" exclaims Wendy. "I don't want to play with William and Wally anyway."

"Me neither," yells Wally, trying to imitate his sister's forcefulness.

In an instant, all three children voluntarily return to their rooms.

"Thank heaven. Now maybe I can enjoy a little peace before supper begins," Mom Shelby desperately hopes.

Go on to Scene 79

Alone in her room, Wendy becomes instantly bored. When bored, Wendy's creativity frequently combines with her high energy to produce disastrous results.

With a plan in mind, Wendy knocks three times on the wall between her room and William's. William responds to the secret signal with three knocks of his own.

Following the terms of their "Three Knock Pact," the now-co-conspirators quietly walk toward the hall, ready to scheme.

Turn to Scene 68

SCENE 80

Mom Shelby kneels down to Wendy's eye level and explains, "Your brother didn't mean to hurt your carriage, Wendy. He was frustrated. He's too young to know what to do when he feels upset. Now let's go together and get your doll carriage and fix it."

Even Mom's eye level approach won't be enough to appease a revenge-seeking Wendy.

"You always take up for Wally. It's not fair. He gets away with everything, even murdering my carriage," Wendy says accusingly.

"Wendy, you know that's not true. I try to be equally fair with all three of you," asserts Mom Shelby defensively.

Wendy has waited for two months to reveal the one terrible secret that will certainly send Wally and William to the gallows.

With revenge in her eyes, Wendy asks, in a tone usually reserved for the word *checkmate,* "What would you do if you discovered that Wally and William killed the Carlsons' cat?"

Turn to Scene 74

SCENE 81

Dad Shelby rushes into Wally's room. Wally stands defiantly over his fallen bookshelf, his book collection littered from one end of the room to the other. Worse, a deep crack now runs the length of the bookshelf.

In a rage, Dad Shelby sets the bookshelf upright, grabs Wally by the hand, and demands, "Put each book back on this shelf while I watch you."

Defiant, Wally picks up one or two books and slowly returns them to their place. Soon realizing that the less quickly he works, the hotter Dad Shelby's blood boils, Wally works more slowly with each passing second.

Understanding that he has punished himself by his declaration to watch Wally until the job is done, Dad's anger is supercharged by his own self-dissatisfaction.

Dad Shelby contains his boiling emotions and remains determined to see this incident out. Wally senses that Dad Shelby is barely in control. Enjoying his newly found power to antagonize Dad Shelby, Wally almost gloats as he methodically replaces his books.

Too inexperienced to keep from crossing the line of safety, Wally knocks a few reshelved books back onto the floor. Frustrated beyond his capacity for self-control, Dad Shelby slaps Wally's hand.

As if by reflex, Wally kicks Dad Shelby in the shins. In retaliation Dad Shelby pushes Wally to the floor. Unfortunately, Wally falls on a stack of books.

"Mom, help!" the youngest cries in his most wounded, betrayed voice.

Mom Shelby enters the scene. There she discovers Dad Shelby standing over the baby of the family. Dad Shelby knows that he won't escape Mom Shelby's doghouse for days.

Second Chance! Turn to Scene 49

But first, see **Power Struggles** (page 237) and **Power Struggles Case Study 2: Bookshelf Waterloo** in the *A–Z Parenting Guide* (page 238).

SCENE 82

Dad Shelby slowly counts to ten. Afterwards, he takes a deep breath and enters Wally's bedroom. As he suspected, books are scattered all over the room. Also, a wide crack stretches the length of the bookshelf.

Defiantly, Wally stands in the corner, obviously waiting for a fight to begin. Dad Shelby refuses to accept the challenge.

"Wally, before you come to supper tonight I expect all of these books to be returned to their shelves," instructs Dad Shelby. Displaying a generous nature, Dad Shelby picks up the bookshelf, puts it in its proper place and leaves the room.

Dumfounded, Wally looks at the task before him. It will take forever to replace these books, he estimates. Disappointed that he missed his opportunity to fight, and frustrated by the task that awaits him, Wally considers his options.

Quickly, he opens his window, drops to the ground and heads toward the Carlsons' house.

Go on to Scene 83

SCENE 83

Wally stops to throw rocks through the Carlsons' fence.

As soon as that challenge is conquered, Wally looks for new targets. Only a few feet away is a giant oak tree.

Wally is young, but he already displays gifted athletic prowess. His first two throws hit the tree squarely in the middle. Encouraged by his success, Wally decides to throw his hardest pitch.

Unfortunately, the rock strays from its mark. A crash is heard. Peering around the tree, Wally sees broken glass all over the ground. Soon his worst fear is confirmed — the window in Mr. Carlson's garage is broken.

Hearing the crash, Mr. Carlson runs into the backyard in time to catch a glimpse of the young offender dashing back into the Shelby home.

With his anger billowing, Mr. Carlson charges to the Shelby's front door and rings the door bell.

Dad Shelby answers the ring and is startled to discover his enraged neighbor at the door.

"Where's that barbaric ruffian of yours?" demands Mr. Carlson.

"Which one?" Dad Shelby responds. "I mean, who are you talking about?"

"Wally, that's who," answers Mr. Carlson. "Your son just broke the window in my garage, and I want to know what you're going to do about it."

"He couldn't have," counters Dad Shelby. "He's in his room putting his books back on the bookshelf."

Dad turns toward Wally's room. One glance at Wally, kneeling, half-hidden from view, convinces Dad Shelby that Mr. Carlson is right.

If you believe that Dad Shelby should say ...

... "You're right, Mr. Carlson. I'll go with you to see the damage," **Turn to Scene 84**

... "Wally, come here this instant. We're going over to Mr. Carlson's house to see what needs to be done," .... **Turn to Scene 85**

SCENE 84

Dad Shelby accompanies the outraged Mr. Carlson to survey the damage to his garage window. Standing by the garage, Mr. Carlson demands, "Now, who is going to pick up this glass?"

Hoping to calm Mr. Carlson's rage, Dad Shelby replies, "I don't mind doing it myself."

As Dad Shelby begins to pick up the glass, Mr. Carlson goes to the Shelby home and returns with the Shelbys' garbage can. Dad is more than a little miffed at Mr. Carlson's enjoyment over torturing him like a wounded animal.

While Dad Shelby searches for pieces of glass, Mr. Carlson points out small fragments that escaped his attention. The entire process becomes more adversarial because of Mr. Carlson's supervisory approach.

Finally, Dad finishes. Mr. Carlson observes, "That's a good job, Shelby. Now you need to search for the rocks Wally threw into my backyard. When you're finished, we'll talk about replacing the window."

That did it! Dad Shelby has finally reached the breaking point. He's not going to bow to Mr. Carlson any more. *But what should I do?* he wonders.

Second Chance! Turn to Scene 83

But first, see **Logical Consequences** (page 217) and
Logical Consequences Case Study 1:
The Hand That Threw the Rock in the *A–Z Parenting Guide* (page 219).

SCENE 85

Wally and Dad Shelby accompany Mr. Carlson to the crime scene. Mr. Carlson points to pieces of the glass scattered around the garage.

"Who's going to pick up this glass? Who's going to pay for the new window? Give me some answers, Shelby," demands Mr. Carlson.

Dad Shelby replies, "Let's ask Wally."

"Wally!" says Mr. Carlson in disbelief. "You're his dad; you make the decisions."

"Mr. Carlson, I didn't break your window. I've learned to be responsible from mistakes I've made similar to Wally's. Wally needs to learn to accept the consequences of his misbehavior," Dad Shelby answers in a firm but kind tone.

"Now Wally," Mr. Shelby begins, "who do you think should pick up the glass and pay for the window?"

"I'll pick up the glass. But it will take me forever to pay for the window," observes a disheartened Wally.

"O.K., Wally. You begin picking up the glass. I'll help find the small pieces. It will take you a long time to pay for the window, but you must pay for at least part of it. We'll talk about money later. Fair enough?" Dad Shelby asks.

"Thanks, Dad," Wally says with sincerity. Wally won't be happy to give up his allowance when the time comes, but the youngster thinks Dad Shelby is the greatest, at least for the moment.

Mr. Carlson backs off almost completely. A slight look of admiration for Dad Shelby appears on his face. But then he remembers — "Who's going to pick up the rocks Wally threw?"

Too late. Dad Shelby heads back toward home, hoping the supper hour will be peaceful . . . .

Turn to Scene 96

SCENE 86

If there's one thing Dad Shelby hates it's to feel humiliated. Having his youngest child trick him into punishing poor William makes Dad Shelby irate.

"Don't you ever try to trick me again," he yells.

The sound of Dad Shelby's voice sends Mom Shelby running toward the emergency site. Mom Shelby knows how unpredictable her husband can become when his vanity is wounded.

When Mom Shelby arrives, she hears Dad Shelby order: "Wally, I want you to bend over and touch the bed. Mr. Belt has a date with Mr. Bottom."

Mom Shelby explodes into the room. Her icy stare meets Dad Shelby's fiery eyes. In an instant, Dad Shelby's flames are extinguished.

"We will settle this matter later. Dad and I need to talk — *right now,*" explains Mom Shelby. After her brazen announcement, the Shelby parents retreat to their bedroom.

Wally feels relieved to be off of the hook. But he's concerned that William and Wendy are disturbed about something.

"Where are you going?" Wally asks his two siblings as they sneak toward their parents' bedroom.

"Shush, Wally," explains Wendy. "There's trouble. We're going to listen."

Turn to Scene 53

SCENE 87

"Wally, breaking William's plane was wrong. It must be replaced. You have just enough money left from the check Grandmother Shelby sent you to pay William for a new one. Also, I want you to stay in your room until dinner. That will give you time to think about your mistake," explains Dad Shelby in his most judicial tone.

Now comes the hard part for Dad Shelby. He could never remember Granddad Shelby apologizing to him, but Dad Shelby decided before having children that he would always try to be forthright with his emotions.

"William," Dad Shelby begins in a halting voice. "I was wrong. I shouldn't have acted without thinking and without talking with you. Sometimes adults make mistakes. I'm sorry."

William feels vindicated. His anger quickly forgotten, William says, almost condescendingly, "Dad, it's all right. Like you said, 'Everyone makes mistakes.'"

Feeling relieved and happy, William goes to his bedroom to play. On the way there, he stops to make a face at Wendy, who is reading in her bedroom. Although Wendy likes to read late at night, she rarely likes to be alone in her room during the afternoon.

Turn to Scene 79

If only Mom Shelby could tell the future, her day might be easier. Unfortunately, she didn't notice a bathtub filled with water. Only moments before, that bathtub had been the scene of a great ocean voyage undertaken by several of Wally's favorite plastic heroes.

Shoes in hand, Wally walks to the bathtub to retrieve his figures. But a slip of the hand and a quick splash later find Wally's shoes afloat in the wavy sea.

Wally pulls his shoes from the water and considers his next move.

Turn to Scene 26

SCENE 89

Now Mom Shelby finds herself in a real jam. She must rush Wendy to school, then return and prepare Wally and herself for their classes.

"Can I take a glass of milk with me in the car?" asks Wendy in her most persuasive voice.

"Wendy, you know we have rules about taking drinks in the car," replies Mom Shelby.

Sensing irresolution, Wendy slides toward the opening, "But I'm thirsty and it will be forever before lunchtime. Please. Please. I'll be extra careful."

"Well, just this once," replies Mom Shelby, regretting her decision already but desperately hoping the risk will work out well.

No such luck.

Not two blocks from her school, Wendy reaches for her book pack and her milk pours into her lap.

"My clothes are soaked!" cries Wendy. "You've got to take me home."

Mom Shelby knows that if she returns home, she'll be late for work and will earn the formidable wrath of her principal.

If you believe Mom Shelby should ...

... refuse to go back home to let Wendy dress, ... **Turn to Scene 90**

... risk being late by rushing back home, ... **Turn to Scene 15**

SCENE 90

Knowing she won't have time to bring Wendy back to Lincoln Elementary School after going home, Mom Shelby declares: "Wendy, you'll have to wash out your clothes in the bathroom and let them dry in class. I can't take you home."

"But Mom!" exclaims Wendy in horror. "Everyone will notice and laugh at me."

"You knew the risk when you brought a glass into the car. You'll just have to manage the best you can," a resolute Mom Shelby counters.

"But you're going home anyway," argues Wendy.

"You know that Wally's school and mine are on opposite ends of town. We cannot come back here. Now that's enough. I'm sorry you spilled your drink. But I know you can handle the problem," says Mom Shelby in an encouraging tone.

Far from pacified, Wendy dives out of the car and slams the door. She exhibits her best "I'm-the-most-abused-child-in-the-world" look as she slowly walks down the sidewalk.

Certain that she made the right decision, Mom Shelby rushes home to prepare for school. She and Wally will need to hurry, but at least Mom Shelby has a reasonable chance of being on time.

For a moment, Mom Shelby basks in the positive assurance of realizing that it was Wendy's problem and not hers. For once, she didn't take the consequences for Wendy's behavior.

But Mom Shelby's positive feelings won't last long. She and Wally arrive home to a new challenge — dressing Wally.

Turn to Scene 31

SCENE 91

Calling the therapist is one of the hardest tasks Mom Shelby has undertaken. To her surprise, the therapist is able to talk briefly with her immediately.

As Mom Shelby explains her family's problems, the counselor doesn't seem surprised. *Maybe she's accustomed to hearing about situations like this,* considers Mom Shelby.

The therapist congratulates Mom Shelby for taking action before problems intensify. She then transfers Mom Shelby's call to the secretary, who makes an appointment. Mom Shelby feels jubilant at first. But then she remembers that the counselor wants to see the entire family. Mom Shelby isn't sure how she will tell Dad Shelby. Nevertheless, she is pleased that she made the call.

Turn to Scene 16

SCENE 92

As much as Mom Shelby wants to ask Wendy about those "terrible things," she believes it's best to walk away from the temptation.

Wendy would have been reluctant to tell Mom Shelby her prize secret under examination. But now that Mom Shelby doesn't appear to want to know, Wendy desperately desires to tell her and casts out the bait: "I suppose you don't care about the Carlsons' dead cat."

Mom Shelby's blood steams. But she's determined not to let Wendy outsmart her this time. Later she can investigate the Carlson Cat Caper.

Arriving in the kitchen, Mom Shelby is thankful that nothing more can go wrong before supper. If only she knew that Wally has sneaked out of his window looking for new adventures.

Turn to Scene 83

"Three!" cries Wendy. "Why me?"

"Because you knew about it and became part of the problem by remaining silent," replies Mom Shelby indignantly.

"Maybe we can get them a new cat," suggests Wally.

"Maybe we can give them Wendy," suggests William sarcastically.

One evil-eyed stare from Mom Shelby tells the children that this is no laughing matter.

If you believe Mom Shelby should ...

... ask her children to confess to the Carlsons, ... **Turn to Scene 77**

... call the Carlsons to explain things, ... **Turn to Scene 95**

... let the issue be buried along with the cat, ... **Turn to Scene 94**

SCENE 94

"**A**ll right, children," sighs an overwhelmed Mom Shelby, "I guess you've learned your lesson and there's nothing we can do to bring the Carlsons' cat to life. I want you to go to your rooms until supper and think about what you've done."

Relieved, the Shelby children flee from the room.

Mom Shelby feels sick inside. She knows she's upset by more than the death of the Carlsons' cat. But she can't put her finger on her dilemma.

Soon Wendy swaggers into the kitchen. She has a superior air about her that Mom Shelby immediately notices and dreads.

"What is it, Wendy?" asks Mom Shelby, not really wanting to hear the answer.

"You see, you were wrong to punish me," explains Wendy as if Mom Shelby should immediately understand.

Perplexed, Mom Shelby inquires, "Why do you think so?"

"Because I kept the boys' secret and you said that silence made me as bad as them. Now you're keeping the secret too, and the Carlsons will never know. You see, Mom, keeping secrets like this can't be wrong. After all, you did it, too," Wendy smugly testifies.

Second Chance! Turn to Scene 93

But first, see **Lying** (page 221) and the **Lying Case Study: Bury More Than the Cat** in the *A–Z Parenting Guide* (page 222).

SCENE 95

Mom Shelby calls the Carlsons to confess about their cat. Mr. Carlson answers the phone and Mom Shelby begins.

"I have terrible news for you. My children accidentally killed your cat," admits Mom Shelby.

"They did what!" shouts Mr. Carlson. "How?"

"They didn't mean to hurt her. William put her in a bag and tried to float her in your fish pond. But they buried her in your backyard by the oak tree," explains Mom Shelby.

Slam — Mr. Carlson pounds the receiver back onto the phone.

In less than a minute, Mom Shelby sees Mr. Carlson enter his tool shed and come out with a shovel.

Second Chance! Turn to Scene 93

But first, see **Respect for Self and Others** (page 242) and
Respect for Self and Others Case Study 3:
Cat Has Children's Tongue in the *A–Z Parenting Guide* (page 243).

Family therapists call it the Arsenic Hour. Mom Shelby, who would never use strong language without cause, claims it's Hell's Hour, for she is convinced that the 60 minutes preceding supper must be a warning of the punishment that awaits those who squander their earthly lives. Before supper begins, everyone demands the cook's total empathy, sympathy and consultation. But no one helps her.

Tonight is no different. As Mom Shelby enters the kitchen, a string of interruptions begins. William and Wendy insist that she settle their dispute over television rights. An evening sales predator calls to hustle a new volume of the *In-Time Nature* series. Wally complains about the menu, then threatens to starve to death before her "boring ol' supper" can be served. As Mom Shelby places the beans on the stove, Dad Shelby seeks comfort for spending an unfruitful day at the office. Even Wizard the cat whines for scraps.

As the stove grows hotter, the kitchen becomes smaller. The entire Shelby family gathers nightly to present the cook — usually Mom Shelby — with their life problems. Ironically, Mom Shelby knows that her day was probably tougher than any of theirs. But no one wants to listen. She's a captive in the kitchen, and everyone has an emergency that she must solve "right now."

As the potatoes begin to boil, so does Mom Shelby's temper. But the food is almost ready and finally her demanding brood can assist her. As Mom Shelby turns to ask for help setting the table, she notices a familiar sign of trouble brewing — silence. The Shelby children and their father have vanished.

Feeling unappreciated, Mom Shelby storms through the house searching for anyone. It doesn't take long to round up the prodigal children. William and Wendy are in the television room. Too addicted to give up the Brainless, they simply turned the volume down, hoping Mom Shelby wouldn't notice them. Wally is entranced in a video game that he has played hundreds of times. And Dad Shelby . . . well, he really knows how to disappear.

Mom Shelby enters the television room. William and Wendy pretend they haven't seen her, concentrating on their program with more than the usual intensity.

"I need help setting the table," announces Mom Shelby.

"I set it last time," proclaims Wendy.

"You did not, I did," interrupts William.

Then, seeing an opportunity open before them, William and Wendy join forces to sacrifice Wally: "Wally never sets the table. He never has to do anything."

Well-trained to scamper toward any possibility, Mom Shelby stalks into Wally's room and declares: "Wally, it's your turn to set the table."

"But, Mom. I can't stop now. It would ruin the game. Besides, it's Wendy's turn," Wally utters without raising his eyes from the video screen. Mom Shelby feels caught. She needs help, but knows she must be forceful and work hard to enlist it.

It will be easier to just do the work myself, she thinks.

If you believe that ...

*... Mom Shelby should take the path of least resistance and
set the table herself,* .... **Turn to Scene 101**

*... Mom Shelby should turn off the video game and
force Wally to help,* .... **Turn to Scene 97**

*... Mom Shelby should gather her children and draw straws
to decide who sets the table,* .... **Turn to Scene 105**

SCENE 97

Mom Shelby doesn't understand video games, and the Shelby children use her ignorance to their advantage. Somehow they've convinced Mom Shelby that to turn off a video game before its completion violates their basic human rights. Having taught her children to complete whatever they begin, Mom Shelby also discovers that she's in unfamiliar territory when insisting that Wally stop in the midst of his activity.

But because Mom Shelby is demanding Wally's help as a matter of principle, her emotions lift her over her usual hurdles.

"Turn that game off this instant, Wally Shelby, and come set the table," exhorts Mom Shelby.

"But, Mom," Wally begins to beg.

"No buts about it. Turn that machine off and come with me," insists Mom Shelby.

Wally hesitates and Mom Shelby reaches down and switches off the machine.

"But, Mom!" Wally wails, as he follows her into the kitchen.

Young Wally has set the table many times. But somehow when he feels unfairly treated (asked to help), he catches a quick case of work amnesia. Recognizing his ailment, Mom Shelby tries to be supportive: "Thanks for helping me, Wally."

Wally doesn't reply. He flits around the kitchen collecting the plates and utensils needed to set the table. Then he storms into the dining room, flings the plates into their approximate places and begins to place the silverware beside the plates.

In a matter of seconds Wally announces: "I'm through. I've done *my work* for the night."

"Stay right there until I look," replies Mom Shelby. Still irritated by her children's lack of desire to help and Wally's tone of voice, Mom Shelby strolls into the dining room to inspect his work.

What she sees is a familiar sight. The plates are placed haphazardly, and the knives and forks are in the wrong places. Mom Shelby isn't sure whether or not Wally's error is intentional. For a moment she considers her response:

If you believe Mom Shelby should ...

... thank Wally for his help and leave the place settings
as they are, ... **Turn to Scene 98**

... tell Wally to redo the settings and do them correctly, ... **Turn to Scene 123**

SCENE 98

"Thank you for your help," Mom Shelby tells Wally with the sincerity of an overworked adult who appreciates any assistance.

Wally looks up with pride, not anticipating the roasting he will take from his siblings for setting the table incorrectly.

Wise in the strategies of allowing nature to take its course and teach its lessons, Mom Shelby permits the table setting to remain.

"Supper!" yells Mom Shelby. "Wash your hands and let's eat," she orders without the slightest belief that any of the six little Shelby hands will be clean when they reach the table.

Dad Shelby appears from his hiding place and Wendy comes in from the television room.

"Where's William?" Mom Shelby asks of the only missing Shelby.

"He went outside to play," Wendy informs her with that poorly hidden joy indigenous to tattletales.

"He what?" exclaims an outraged Mom Shelby. "William knew that we were about to eat."

"He said he wasn't hungry," Wendy adds, to supercharge her mom's anger.

With that extra information propelling her, Mom Shelby charges to the front door. Looking outside, she cannot see William, but she's certain that he's within earshot.

If you believe Mom Shelby should ...

*... demand that William join them immediately so supper
won't be ruined,* .... **Turn to Scene 99**

... eat without him and let him miss supper, ... **Turn to Scene 103**

92

SCENE 99

"**W**illiam! William Shelby, supper is ready. Come here this instant," yells Mom Shelby.

William hears her, but he can tell by her tone that she isn't angry enough yet for him to respond. William continues to play "ghost in the graveyard" with his friends.

"William Shelby! Can you hear me?" Mom Shelby demands.

One of William's friends stops playing and dares him: "You'd better do what your Mommy wants you to do, William baby."

William feels trapped between his fear of Mom Shelby and his desire to meet his friend's challenge.

"William Shelby, you'd better come here before I count to ten," threatens Mom Shelby.

William knows that Mom Shelby's voice has now reached its most dangerous tone. And worse, Mom Shelby counts to ten only during emotional emergencies. No one in the Shelby house knows what will happen if she ever reaches ten. But everyone assumes that some things are best left unexplored.

"One . . . two . . . three . . . four . . . five . . . six . . . seven . . . William, this is your last chance," Mom Shelby announces, feeling just as anxious as William about what will happen if she reaches ten.

"Eight . . . nine . . . I'm warning you, William Shelby," threatens Mom Shelby. But William doesn't budge. His friends remain frozen. They've never heard a child's parent reach ten.

"Ten!" yells Mom Shelby.

If you believe Mom Shelby should ...

... *close the door and begin eating supper without William,* ... **Turn to Scene 103**

... *charge out the door and force William to come into the house,* . . . . **Turn to Scene 100**

SCENE 100

Mom Shelby charges out of the house. Although she wasn't originally sure where William and his friends were playing, when angry her parental sixth sense directs her straight toward the culprit.

Seeing Mom Shelby rushing through the yard is more than enough to spark the retreat of William's friends. Suddenly, the youngster who stayed with his friends to stand up to Mom Shelby is left alone to confront her wrath.

"William, when I get through with you, there won't be enough of you left to feed the cat," yells Mom Shelby. Poor Mom Shelby knows that she's not as angry as she sounds, but she believes a show of force to be necessary.

William, however, is really frightened. He's never heard Mom Shelby this angry and he's not sure what she's about to do. In a panic he yells to his friends, "Wait for me! I'm coming with you."

With that, William runs up the block to catch up with friends, who want no part of him.

For Mom Shelby, an incident that began as an annoying distraction has grown into a major confrontation. But what will happen next is beyond her imagination. After all, she's never reached ten before.

Second Chance! Turn to Scene 99

But first, see **Natural Consequences** (page 225) and
Natural Consequences Case Study 3:
7, 8, 9, 10! Now You've Had It! in the *A–Z Parenting Guide* (page 228).

*G*etting help from this family is just not worth the effort, decides Mom Shelby. As she walks back toward the kitchen, she feels more unappreciated than ever.

Although Mom Shelby may appear to be in a trance, she is creating a soliloquy worthy of a Shakespearean tragedy: *All day I work for this family. I awaken the children, help them get to school, teach all day, then come home and work some more. Dad Shelby claims to be liberated, but he sure isn't helping very much. No one helps. And no one appreciates how much I do for them and how little I do for myself.*

Mechanically, Mom Shelby sets the table, then by habit walks into the television room and announces that dinner is ready.

"William went outside to play," Wendy informs her.

"But he knew we were about to eat," whines a defeated Mom Shelby.

Continuing her journey to locate people willing to eat her dinner, Mom Shelby notices that Wally is still held captive by his video game.

"Supper, Wally," Mom Shelby announces.

"Just a minute, Mom. I can't stop now," replies Wally.

Mom Shelby has entered that land that lies beyond the last straw. In these moments anger no longer disguises hurt. Mom Shelby summons Dad Shelby to supper, but she no longer cares whether or not he arrives.

Finally, Wendy, Wally and Dad Shelby appear and sit down at the dinner table.

"Where's William?" inquires Dad Shelby in a tone that implies that it's Mom Shelby's responsibility to get everyone to the table.

"He's playing," Wendy eagerly explains.

By this time Dad Shelby and Wendy sense that Mom Shelby is in no mood to face conflict. Dad Shelby tries to help.

"Whose turn is it to say the blessing?" he inquires.

No one answers. Dad Shelby is too slow to volunteer, and Mom Shelby recites the routine Shelby blessing with an obvious lack of enthusiasm.

The family begins dinner in a silence broken only by Wally's rambling about his video game accomplishments. Suddenly, Wally stops and asks, "Why do we always have to eat these dumb ol' beans? They're already cold."

Afterwards, her family might argue about whether any warning signs preceded Mom Shelby's explosion. But her few words carried with them her feelings of hurt, anger and outrage: "If you don't like supper, cook it yourself! I don't care if any of you ever eats again!"

As she finishes her last words, Mom Shelby storms from the table in tears.

If you believe Mom Shelby should ...

*... stay in her bedroom until Dad Shelby comes to talk
with her,* .... **Turn to Scene 120**

*... pull herself together and tell her family exactly
what is bothering her,* .... **Turn to Scene 102**

... call a counselor to talk about her life challenges, ... **Turn to Scene 117**

SCENE 102

Mom Shelby pulls her emotions together and returns to the supper table. She's greeted by awkward silence. Everyone is pretending that nothing happened. If anything is to be said, Mom Shelby will have to initiate the discussion. She begins.

"I'm sorry I blew up at you all. But I've worked really hard today, and it seems all that I hear are complaints. No one has lifted a finger to help," she explains. Her comments strike home.

"I'm sorry, Mom. We'll do better," Wendy volunteers.

"Yeah, I'm sorry too," says Wally, obviously unsure why he's apologizing.

"And that goes for me too," says a repentant Dad Shelby. "We'll all carry our share of the load from now on," adds Dad Shelby.

Mom Shelby doesn't believe them for a moment! But it is good to see her family show concern.

On some days, life never becomes easier. Mom Shelby's good feelings end after she finishes her discussion. She notices that William has still not joined them for supper.

"Where's William?" Mom Shelby asks about the only missing Shelby.

"He went outside to play," Wendy informs her with that poorly hidden joy tattletales exude.

"He what?" exclaims an outraged Mom Shelby. "William knew that we were about to eat."

"He said he wasn't hungry," Wendy adds to supercharge her mom's anger.

With that extra information propelling her, Mom Shelby charges to the front door. Looking outside, she cannot see William, but she's certain that he's within earshot.

If you believe Mom Shelby should ...

> ... *demand that William join them immediately so supper*
> *won't be ruined,* . . . . **Turn to Scene 99**

> ... *eat without him and let him miss supper,* . . . . **Turn to Scene 103**

SCENE 103

Mom Shelby returns to the table without William. Dad Shelby, displaying a keen grasp of the obvious, notes, "William didn't come with you." Then he adds, "Why don't you go get him?"

Fortunately for Dad Shelby, Mom Shelby doesn't return an equally obvious comment. After all, Dad Shelby loves to have the family eat together, although he rarely helps herd the children to the table.

"I'm not going to ruin my supper and everyone else's by chasing William down. He knows it's supper time. I'm tired of playing 'Fetch Me' every night before supper," explains Mom Shelby.

"But what if he misses supper?" inquires Wally.

"Then he'll get hungry, won't he?" Mom Shelby replies without bitterness.

Dad Shelby gives a look that respects Mom Shelby's logic but also suggests that a growing boy might starve if a meal is missed. Wendy looks for holes in Mom Shelby's plan.

"William will just eat potato chips and fill up on junk. Sounds like a good bargain to me," Wendy evaluates.

"You're welcome to the same deal, Wendy. Besides, there are no potato chips in the house. I let all of the junk food run out and bought fruit instead," Mom Shelby reveals.

Dad Shelby squirms. He respects Mom Shelby's stance, but he was planning to watch sports on television tonight. *How can he watch without eating?* he ponders.

Turn to Scene 126

SCENE 104

Mom Shelby decides to lay into William: "You never have consideration for anyone else's feelings, William Shelby. You left this house knowing good and well that supper was almost ready. Now you take this food and go warm it up and don't ever be late for dinner in this house again or you won't eat at all."

Knowing how to win such fights, William calmly says, "I'm not hungry anyway. I'm going to do my homework. Please don't bother me."

William exits, leaving Mom Shelby more angry than before. But now there is no one to vent her frustrations on. No one, that is, except for Wizard the cat, who has just had the misfortune of jumping on the table to forage for food.

With the day's frustration raging, Mom Shelby hurls a hotpad at the feline. The missile misses Wizard but terrifies him. The cat streaks away, toppling over a half-filled glass of milk that Wally never bothered to return to the kitchen. Mom Shelby is too numb to move.

Second Chance! Turn to Scene 126

But first, see **Natural Consequences** (page 225) and
Natural Consequences Case Study 4:
One Entrée from Victory in the *A–Z Parenting Guide* (page 229).

SCENE 105

"You three come here this instant," orders an outraged Mom Shelby. "If you don't work, you don't eat in the Shelby house."

William, Wendy and Wally file into the dining room. They know that when Mom Shelby gets on one of her "don't work, don't eat" tirades they'd better cooperate. With any luck, her vigilance will last only a day or two and then she and Dad Shelby will leave them alone.

"Each of you pick a straw," Mom Shelby instructs as she holds three pieces of paper in her hand.

"How can you tell if you win?" inquires William.

"Just draw. Everyone wins," Mom Shelby retorts.

"I have the long one. I won!" exclaims Wally.

"Yes, Wally. You won the right to pour drinks for everyone. Wendy, you have the short straw, so you can put the food on the table. And William, you won the right to set the table," informs Mom Shelby as if she were a game show host.

"That's not fair," complains William. "What are *you* going to do?"

If he could have, William would have intercepted those words before they reached Mom Shelby's ears. But it's too late. The Shelby kids brace themselves for the storm.

If you believe Mom Shelby should ...

... *give William a long glance and say nothing,* .... **Turn to Scene 106**

... *give the Shelby kids a talk on who does what
in the Shelby household,* .... **Turn to Scene 107**

SCENE 106

Some people call it the "evil eye." But by any name, every child knows the *look* a parent gives that shows disbelief, disgust, warning, punishment, correction and coercion.

Wendy calls it the Shelby Stare. It's saved for those few moments in life when Mom Shelby knows she's absolutely in the right. This is one of those moments.

William tries to repent before the Shelby Stare begins. "I'm sorry. I know how hard you and Dad work," confesses William. But Mom Shelby is unrelenting. William looks away, but the stare can be felt as well as seen.

Just to show that the Shelby Stare didn't totally defeat him, William adds, "Just don't give me the speech."

Everyone knows the long, boring speech that William means. Mom Shelby gives the drawn-out speech about who works hardest in the household to wear out her opposition. The Shelby Stare works more like a space gun that dematerializes unappreciative children.

The Shelby children quickly reform, set the table, and file to the dinner table. They're not about to cause problems now. Or are they?

Turn to Scene 108

SCENE 107

The Shelby kids aren't sure how many times they've heard the "Work Speech," but it seems like a nightmare they can't escape. In a few years, the Shelby children will be old enough to deflect the speech by reciting it word for word before Mom Shelby can begin. But for now, they must wait out the storm.

"When was the last time you cleaned out a toilet, William Shelby? Don't you look so smug, Wendy Shelby. When was the last time you fixed your own school lunch or washed the kitchen floor? And Wally Shelby, I don't see you fighting to vacuum the living room rugs or to wash the windows in the den. Who do you think does all of this work?" Mom Shelby orates.

Although Mom Shelby's "Work Speech" is always composed of a series of questions, her technique shouldn't be confused with the Socratic method. In time, Mom Shelby provides not only the questions, but also the answers.

"I'll tell you who does the work and who does the play in this house . . ." she continues.

Beaten down by the speech, the Shelby children look like deflated blow-up dolls. Mercifully, a timer goes off in the kitchen and the speech ends.

Wally and Wendy stare at William. How *could* he have provoked *the speech* once again? The children quickly set the table. Thank heaven supper is beginning, everyone agrees.

Turn to Scene 108

SCENE 108

The Shelby family sits at the dinner table, finally ready to begin dinner.

As usual, Wally is babbling about anything that flashes through his mind. Dad Shelby tries to gain the family's attention in order to make plans for the weekend, but Wally continues to interrupt.

Irritated, Dad Shelby observes, "Wally, you haven't eaten anything on your plate. Be quiet and eat."

Wally begins to play with his food, moving things around on his plate but not eating anything. After a few moments, Dad Shelby intervenes again: "There are people starving all over the world, and you won't eat anything."

William and Wendy look down nervously. They know where this "starving" discussion usually ends up. Although they enjoy seeing Wally get into trouble, they don't relish having their evening ruined. Wally continues to play with his food and Dad Shelby's temper rises.

If you believe Dad Shelby should ...

... give Wally a whack and send him to his room
   if he refuses to eat, ...**Turn to Scene 109**

... urge Wally to eat supper by offering him dessert, ...**Turn to Scene 110**

... ignore Wally and let him choose whether or not to eat, ...**Turn to Scene 111**

SCENE 109

Wally looks determined not to eat. Dad Shelby is as determined to make him eat. Somehow, William, Wendy and Mom Shelby know to stay out of this conflict or Dad Shelby's anger will shift to whomever interferes.

"Wally, I want you to clean that plate. Your mother spent a long time preparing your food and it's not going to be wasted," Dad Shelby preaches.

"I'm not hungry," Wally responds in an attempt to forge a compromise.

"Too bad. That's good food and you need to eat to be healthy," instructs Dad Shelby.

Now that Dad Shelby has thrown away the possibility of compromise, Wally senses that he's in control of the situation. He can eat and Dad Shelby will calm down, or he can continue to play with his food and Dad Shelby will explode. Their confrontation is no longer about eating supper. It's now about power.

Wally rearranges his food slowly to torment Dad Shelby. Whether intentional or not, Wally topples a few of his beans onto the tablecloth.

"That's it!" Dad Shelby yells. He jumps up from the table and grabs Wally by the arm. With a whack on Wally's rear, Dad Shelby orders, "Go to your room and stay there until I tell you to come out. You've got to learn to respect other people's work. Mom Shelby spent a long time cooking this supper."

Dad Shelby escorts Wally to his room. The sounds of Wally's crying reach the dinner table before Dad Shelby returns.

Mom Shelby hates these supper episodes. Equally, she dislikes Dad Shelby's use of her work in preparing supper to justify fighting with Wally. But she feels powerless to interfere.

When Dad Shelby returns to the table, no one looks up. Dinner has been taken hostage by silence.

Finally, Mom Shelby can't tolerate the tension. She throws her napkin on the table and stalks away from the table.

What began as a gentle Shelby dinner has ended in a war with total casualties. Nothing has been won. And no one knows what will happen at supper tomorrow night.

Second Chance! Turn to Scene 108
But first, see **Natural Consequences** (page 225) and
Natural Consequences Case Study 2:
Eat Beans or Be Beaten in the *A–Z Parenting Guide* (page 227).

SCENE 110

"I'm not hungry," Wally moans in his most pitiful voice.

"But you need to eat," Dad Shelby responds. "Don't you want to grow up to be as strong as your Uncle Clarence Shelby? Don't forget — he played professional baseball."

Wally doesn't look up. He sticks out his lower lip and plays with his food. William and Wendy are irritated — they know how this scene usually plays out.

"Wally, if you eat your supper I'll take you out to the Banana Split for ice cream," offers Dad Shelby.

Usually William and Wendy cash in on the dessert deal, but tonight they're too rankled to see Wally get what he wants by manipulating Dad Shelby once again.

"You're such a spoiled brat," Wendy yells at Wally.

"Am not," defends Wally.

"Are too," joins William.

"Am not," Wally says in a manner that clearly begs for Mom or Dad Shelby's intervention.

For Wendy, that's the last straw. She picks up a fork full of beans and slings them at Wally. In retaliation Wally sails a roll into Wendy's chest.

"Enough!" yells Mom Shelby. Dad Shelby and William look on in horror. Clearly Wendy and Wally just misbehaved in ways that William could only imagine. And Dad Shelby, well, he may never understand what provoked this outbreak.

Second Chance! Turn to Scene 108

But first, see **Permissiveness** (page 232) and
Permissiveness Case Study 3:
The Banana Splits the Children in the *A–Z Parenting Guide* (page 235).

Wally looks determined not to eat. Dad Shelby is as determined to make him eat. But Dad Shelby has been down that road before. Dad Shelby recalls the occasions when he tried to force William and Wendy to eat. Dinner always ended in an angry, tear-filled confrontation.

Although Dad Shelby's inclination is to use force, he decides, "If Wally doesn't eat, then he'll be the one to go hungry. No snacks tonight."

William senses that Dad Shelby is backing off. At first William didn't want to witness a major confrontation, but now the joys of a fine fight seem appealing. Maybe he can lure Dad Shelby back into the fray. "Gee, Dad," he says, "how come Wally doesn't have to eat anything?"

Dad Shelby understands William's goal and sidesteps him.

"None of you has to eat. In fact, *don't* eat and there will be more for me," Dad Shelby says, making a joke.

"That's not fair. You used to make *us* eat. Wally is a spoiled brat," declares William.

"Your dad has learned from experience," Mom Shelby proudly announces. "Sometimes you have to let people make their own decisions."

"You mean I don't have to eat this stuff?" asks Wally.

"It's up to you, Wally. The next meal is breakfast and there will be no snacks tonight," Dad Shelby announces.

"But I might get hungry," interjects Wally.

"That's up to you," replies Dad Shelby. Mom Shelby beams, and Dad Shelby knows this is one of his finest moments. Now if he can only say no to snacks!

Turn to Scene 112

SCENE 112

Mom Shelby feels wonderful that supper has gone so well. "Come on, Wendy, let's clear the table and wash the dishes," she urges in a friendly tone.

"Let's not," Wendy counters with surprising force.

"Why, Wendy? We always clear the table and wash dishes together," notes a startled Mom Shelby.

"That's right. We always do. And what do William, Wally and Dad do?" questions Wendy.

"We watch sports on television," Wally replies with an honesty no one but Wendy wants to hear.

"Well, that's not *all* we do," Dad Shelby struggles to explain. "We take out the trash and mow the grass."

"When was the last time *you* took out the trash?" challenges Mom Shelby.

"Why can't I mow the grass? I can cut it as well as William. Why can't I take out the trash instead of washing dishes? Let William wash dishes for once. Why can't we be like other families?" quizzes Wendy.

"Who have you been talking to?" questions Dad Shelby.

"I don't think that matters," counters Mom Shelby. "Wendy has a good point. The males in this family should be working just as hard as the females."

Clearly this discussion covers new territory in the Shelby family. Both Mom and Dad Shelby were raised in traditional homes. Dad Shelby prides himself on how much more work in the home he does than Grandpa Shelby ever did.

"But I *do* work hard," suggests Dad Shelby. "I do most of the laundry and all of the car and house maintenance."

"I know, but William and Wally don't even know how to turn on the dishwasher. They're helpless. Unless they become millionaires or marry slaves, they won't be prepared for adult life," suggests Mom Shelby.

"But I say if it's not broken, don't fix it," declares Dad Shelby. "I don't want to be unreasonable, but this job division has worked for many years without complaint."

"But times change, dear," Mom Shelby begins. "We're a different family from the way we were five years ago. I've gone back to work. The kids are big enough to learn life skills."

"But I'm not going to wash clothes and dishes. What would my friends say?" asks William.

"They'd probably say that you're an independent young man," replies Mom Shelby. "You need to learn to take care of yourself."

"I've heard enough," proclaims Dad Shelby. "Until I see a good reason to change, we'll keep our chores the same."

At that moment Mom Shelby and Wally break into a fit of laughter. There in the entrance to the dining room stands Wendy dressed like Abraham Lincoln. Dressed in a black suit, Wendy sports a beard left over from Halloween and a top hat. "If I'm going to live in this family, I'm not going to be a girl. From now on I'm Warren Wendy Shelby, the next candidate for cave man."

If you believe Dad Shelby should ...

... Let Wendy know that job assignments are no laughing matter in the Shelby household, ...**Turn to Scene 116**

... See how important jobs are to Wendy and make some changes, ...**Turn to Scene 113**

SCENE 113

Seeing Wendy dressed up even makes Dad Shelby laugh: "I guess I've finally seen a good reason to change," he acknowledges. "All right, boys, let's clear the table and wash the dishes. Warren Wendy Shelby just brought in the new age."

"Not so fast," Mom Shelby directs. "Wendy and I don't want this to be a one-night change. Let's find a way to distribute jobs that will allow everyone to eventually do each chore."

"Why don't we just draw straws?" suggest William.

"There are too many jobs for that," explains Mom Shelby. "But maybe we can put slips naming all of the jobs that need to be shared into a jar and take turns drawing."

"Sounds good to me," affirms Dad Shelby. "Would you be willing to write out the job slips, Mom?"

She's already writing. The jar fills in seconds and Mom Shelby announces: "Time to draw. Dad, please draw first."

"Me!" exclaims Dad Shelby. "I thought this was just for the children."

"Of course not. We all need to help around the house. Please take the first turn," urges Mom Shelby.

Dad Shelby draws *Clean out toilets and bathtubs* and cries, "No way!"

If you believe Dad Shelby should ...

... *refuse to do a job he doesn't want to complete,* .... **Turn to Scene 115**

... *accept the job,* .... **Turn to Scene 114**

... *share his feelings with his family,* .... **Turn to Scene 187**

SCENE 114

"If you believe that cleaning bathtubs and toilets is too demeaning for you to do, who do you believe should clean them? Pick one of us," Mom Shelby challenges.

Dad Shelby looks at each family member and knows that Mom Shelby has made her point.

"I'll help you, Dad," Wally offers in an enthusiastic voice.

Wally's offer makes the task seem less offensive.

"All right, I'll do it. But William and Wendy, do your homework as soon as your chores are completed," orders Dad Shelby. He rarely talks about homework, but giving a command seems important at a time when his role in the family seems challenged.

Mom Shelby looks at her husband and says, "Thanks, dear. We need some peace and quiet together. Why don't you and I wash dishes?" Dad Shelby likes the idea. He needs to talk and being alone with Mom Shelby seems perfect.

Turn to Scene 128

"If you believe that cleaning bathtubs and toilets is too nasty for you to do, then who do you think *should* do it? Pick one of us," challenges Mom Shelby.

Dad Shelby hates to be backed into a corner. Particularly, he hates *this* corner because he knows that whatever he says next will be wrong.

"I don't think anyone should have to do that type of work. But we can't afford to pay anyone to work in our house. I work a long day at the office. I just don't want to mess with this kind of job when I come home," Dad Shelby explains in a conciliatory tone. Little does he know that such a seemingly innocent comment will enrage Mom Shelby.

"So who doesn't work hard? Do you want to start comparing job lists? I'll be glad to. Start writing down all that you accomplish during a day and I'll write down what I do. Let's compare notes," dares Mom Shelby.

The children look horrified. They're not accustomed to hearing disputes handled confrontationally. Dad Shelby feels humiliated. For Mom Shelby the issue may be respect and fairness in job distribution, but Dad Shelby just wants to save face.

"I'm not doing toilets or bathtubs, and that's final," declares Dad Shelby.

"That's fine. Then I resign as maid. We'll let the whole house stink to high heaven," shouts back Mom Shelby.

Second Chance! Turn to Scene 113

But first, see **Communications** (page 197) and
Communications Case Study 2:
You Do the Dirty Work in the *A–Z Parenting Guide* (page 199).

"**W**endy, take off those stupid-looking clothes this instant. We're talking about serious issues. This is no laughing matter," announces Dad Shelby.

Wendy takes off the beard and clothes, dropping them on the floor.

"Pick your clothes up immediately. That's the problem here. People don't take care of their belongings," preaches Dad Shelby.

"*That's* not the problem," mumbles Wendy.

"What did you say, young lady?" challenges Dad Shelby.

"Nothing, never mind," grumbles Wendy.

"She said *that's* not the problem, and I agree," Mom Shelby notes with conviction.

"Don't you side with the children against me," Dad Shelby warns.

"I'm not siding. We're trying to talk about important family challenges," clarifies Mom Shelby.

"We're not talking about anything. I'm telling you that nothing is changing in the Shelby household. If you don't like our home, pack your bags," commands Dad Shelby. With that parting shot, Dad Shelby walks out of the house and slams the door.

"Let's pack our bags," Wendy suggests.

This time, no one laughed.

Second Chance! Turn to Scene 112

But first, see **Family Meetings** (page 204) and the
Family Meetings Case Study:
Flight of the Neanderthal in the *A–Z Parenting Guide* (page 205).

Mom Shelby throws herself on the bed. Her chest cavity feels empty, as if she's about to implode. *No one cares. No one listens,* she reflects.

But then she remembers the family counselor who helped her earlier. Maybe she would understand. Mom Shelby dials the office, hoping the counselor has night hours. Her secretary answers.

"How can I help you?" inquires the secretary.

"I'm just calling in hopes that I can talk with the counselor, if she is free for a moment," explains Mom Shelby.

"I'm sorry, but she's in sessions until ten o'clock tonight. She will return your call tonight if it's an emergency. Otherwise, she can call you tomorrow," the secretary offers.

Suddenly Mom Shelby feels embarrassed. *I'm a grown woman and I can't even handle my own problems,* she thinks.

If you believe that Mom Shelby should ...

... *hang up and handle the situation herself,* .... **Turn to Scene 118**

... *ask for the therapist to return the call,* .... **Turn to Scene 119**

SCENE 118

"That's all right," Mom Shelby explains. "It's not an emergency. Don't bother the doctor. I'll get back in touch later."

"It's really no bother. Calling back is part of the doctor's work. She really doesn't mind," says the secretary.

"No. Everything will be fine. Really. Thank you," answers Mom Shelby before she hangs up.

Once off the phone, life seems more hopeless. Mom Shelby still feels unappreciated. Now, there's no one to talk with about her challenges. *How could life get any worse?* she ponders.

Then Mom Shelby hears the sound of Dad Shelby walking up to the bedroom door. He knocks and then belts out, "What the hell is the matter with you?"

I guess that's how life can grow worse, Mom Shelby reflects.

Second Chance! Turn to Scene 117

But first, see **Family Therapy** (page 206) and the
Family Therapy Case Study: Hopeless in Center City
in the *A–Z Parenting Guide* (page 206).

SCENE 119

"**Y**es, I'd love to have the counselor call me, but it's not an emergency. I'm just feeling down about things," explains Mom Shelby. "This is Mrs. Shelby."

"Oh, yes. I'll have the doctor call first thing tomorrow morning," the secretary replies.

"Thanks so much," Mom Shelby says with relief. "I feel better already. Just remember that if possible she needs to call before 8 o'clock."

"I'm sure she'll do her best. But I know if she cannot reach you early, she'll call tomorrow night," replies the secretary.

When Mom Shelby finally returns the phone to the receiver, she notices that her chest seems filled. She has hope — someone who will listen and understand.

Mom Shelby rolls off the bed. "Now I can face supper," she thinks.

She returns to the dinner table, which is now empty, and calls, "Let's finish supper."

Relieved that Mom Shelby seems O.K., everyone runs to the table.

Turn to Scene 108

SCENE 120

Mom Shelby lies on her bed sobbing. She feels totally empty inside, as if she might implode. "No one cares about me. All I do is slave for other people," she reflects.

The longer Mom Shelby cries, the angrier she grows at her family and the more depressed she feels.

Innocently, Dad Shelby approaches the bedroom door and knocks. With a touch of levity he begins: "You must have had a tough day, to say the least."

Less said would have been better, thinks Mom Shelby. She's indignant at Dad Shelby's humor and understatement. This wasn't a "tough" day; this was an *awful* day. And besides, a bad day isn't the problem. Her family is.

"Would you like to talk about it?" offers Dad Shelby.

If you believe Mom Shelby should ...

... put aside her initial anger at Dad Shelby and talk, ... **Turn to Scene 121**

... refuse to talk to Dad Shelby until he recognizes
the seriousness of her feelings, ... **Turn to Scene 122**

SCENE 121

Mom Shelby's feelings tell her to refuse to talk to Dad Shelby. At least now her depression allows her to provide herself with sympathy and comfort. After she begins a conversation with Dad Shelby there is no guarantee where she may end up. Besides, she considers, she shouldn't talk to him until he displays more sensitivity for her situation. Maybe her silence will teach Dad Shelby a lesson.

Fortunately, Mom Shelby's memory runs deeper than her feelings. *But I just can't stand another one of those standoffs. Neither of us talking to the other, just going through the motions of marriage.*

Having waved her own red flag, Mom Shelby invites Dad Shelby to talk. She begins, "It's hard to start, but I'll try. I feel so unappreciated when I come home from work and no one helps with the housework. I feel hurt that my family takes me for granted . . . ."

After twenty minutes, Dad Shelby emerges from the room. In moments, the Shelby kids begin warming supper and decorating the table. Finally, Wally comes to the door and announces, "Supper's ready. Come and get it."

Whatever the Shelbys discussed certainly seemed to have worked. Mom Shelby looks totally rejuvenated as she walks to the dinner table. Maybe her problems are over for the day. Or maybe they're not.

Turn to Scene 108

Mom Shelby feels torn between her anger at her family and her desire not to enter a cold war with Dad Shelby. It's not as if this scenario hasn't occurred before. Sometimes, when Mom Shelby becomes angriest, the only way she seems to be able to make the family think about her needs is to drop out of their lives.

During these periods, Mom Shelby completes all of her chores and responsibilities, but she becomes noncommunicative. As a result, Dad Shelby usually becomes much more sensitive, trying not to tread accidentally on Mom Shelby's feelings. Eventually the two discuss their problems, and life goes better for a while.

Mom Shelby doesn't like these periods of cold war, but she knows they work. In some ways, she wants to open up and talk about things now. But maybe Dad Shelby isn't ready to listen. Maybe he needs to be impressed with the seriousness of her feelings. Mom Shelby struggles to decide whether to talk with him or ignore him.

"Honey," Dad Shelby entreats, "I really want to talk with you. Can we talk?"

Something in Dad Shelby's voice strikes a negative chord in Mom Shelby. She replies, "No, everything is just fine. I don't need to talk."

Mom Shelby hears Dad Shelby walk away from the door. Now she's unhappy, but she imagines that he is equally miserable. *Some families might think this is a tough way to communicate. But it works for the Shelbys,* she thinks. Alone, she grows more depressed. But she's sure that this is the best way to solve this challenge.

Second Chance! Turn to Scene 120

But first, see **Communications** (page 197) and
Communications Case Study 1: Cold Warrior Attacks
in the *A–Z Parenting Guide* (page 198).

SCENE 123

"Wally Shelby," says Mom Shelby. "You know how to set the table correctly. Come in here and do it right."

Wally waddles into the dining room and innocently asks: "What's wrong?"

"You know very well what's wrong, young man. Now set this table as it should be," orders Mom Shelby.

"But this *is* the right way," maintains Wally in an unconvincing tone.

"It's not the way I taught you. Now, put the knives to the right of the plates and the forks to the left of the plates," instructs Mom Shelby.

"Oh, that's right," Wally offers, as if startled by insight.

Mom Shelby watches Wally, then notes, "That's not the way you're supposed to put napkins on the table. Fold them and place them under the forks."

"I don't want to do it that way," complains Wally.

"Just do it. And when you're finished, bring in all of the food from the kitchen," orders Mom Shelby.

Frustrated by his repeated failures and the new assignment, Wally sobs.

If you believe Mom Shelby should ...

... ignore Wally and insist that he do his work correctly, ... **Turn to Scene 124**

... offer to do the tasks together, ... **Turn to Scene 125**

"That's enough crying, Wally Shelby. If you did your work right, you wouldn't need to cry. Now place the napkins correctly and put the food on the table," orders Mom Shelby.

Wally feels totally incompetent. He tries to figure out how to fold the napkins so they'll fit under the forks. But with Mom Shelby watching over him, he becomes self-conscious. Nevertheless, he takes a stab at folding the napkins.

"That's not right!" corrects Mom Shelby, grabbing a napkin and showing Wally the proper way to fold it. "It's so simple, if you just think about it. Now you fold the rest of them."

At her new command, Wally flings the napkins at Mom Shelby and yells: "Leave me alone! I hate you." The napkins flutter to the floor, but Wally's message strikes home.

"Come back here, Wally," Mom Shelby shrieks. But the only response is the sound of the door slamming.

"Why is he so stubborn?" Mom Shelby ponders. "Sometimes he makes me so angry. What gets into him, anyway?"

Second Chance! Turn to Scene 123

But first, see **Chores** (page 196) and the
Chores Case Study: Forks to the Left!
in the *A–Z Parenting Guide* (page 196).

SCENE 125

"**W**ally, I guess I've overwhelmed you a little, haven't I?" Mom Shelby asks.

Wally's not sure what she means, but he's certain that he likes her tone of voice.

"I appreciate your trying to help. Let's work on the table together — what do you say?" invites Mom Shelby.

"O.K.," says Wally, showing a bit of energy once again.

"Let's do the first napkin together. Then I'll race you around the table to see who finishes first. But if we're not neat, we'll need to go back and do it over," Mom Shelby challenges.

Having fun always appeals to Wally Shelby. Add competition to fun and Wally springs to life. Before Mom Shelby knows it, the table is set and Wally is beaming.

"Grand job, Wally. That was fun," Mom Shelby notes. Wally's face shows his agreement.

Turn to Scene 108

SCENE 126

At that very moment, the door slams and William runs to the table. By this time, everyone else has almost finished eating.

"Why didn't anyone call me?" William innocently asks, in order to shift attention away from his error. Holding her temper, Mom Shelby refuses to reply.

William sits down and begins to eat. Soon he makes an obvious observation: "Everything's cold."

Should Mom Shelby, who has completed her supper ...

... tell William exactly what she thinks of his being late and
require him to heat up his own supper, ... **Turn to Scene 104**

... say nothing and leave the table, ... **Turn to Scene 127**

SCENE 127

Mom Shelby bites her tongue and walks toward the kitchen. Dad Shelby supports Mom Shelby's plan: "William, you know how to use the microwave. Warm up your food if you wish to."

"Me? Since when is it my job to cook supper?" demands William.

Now Dad Shelby's anger begins to rise. But Mom Shelby has returned and picks up the conversation: "William, it's up to you. Warm it up or not; it doesn't matter to me."

"I'm not going to warm up anything," declares William. He walks to the kitchen and searches the cabinets for fast food. Finding none he grabs a pear, returns to the table and sulks.

Mom and Dad Shelby ignore William. Wendy doesn't: "This is great food, Mom. You really know how to cook."

William can stand no more. Having swallowed only his pride thus far, William takes his plate and places it in the microwave.

"Something's on fire!" yells Wally a few minutes later.

William runs to the kitchen and brings back a supper in various stages of burn damage.

Mom and Dad Shelby hide a smile as William pretends his supper is in perfect shape and eats the charred remains.

Enjoying every moment of William's learning experience, Mom Shelby muses to herself, *I bet William won't stray away from home tomorrow night. But if he does, finally he will take the consequences instead of the entire family.*

Turn to Scene 112

SCENE 128

Finding time to spend alone provides a tough challenge for Mom and Dad Shelby. Washing dishes together becomes a refuge from the children. If the Shelby youngsters wander into the kitchen, Mom and Dad Shelby offer to put them to work. Such propositions send the Shelby kids scampering out of sight.

Parents' peaceful times always end quickly. After completing kitchen chores, Mom Shelby tracks down the Shelby children to see if they have any homework. As expected, she discovers them riveted to the Brainless.

Mom Shelby interrupts, "Who has homework tonight?"

"I never have homework," Wally chuckles.

Wendy joins in, "I did mine in school."

"What about you, William?" asks Mom Shelby.

"I don't have any," William blurts out.

"Are you sure, William?" Mom Shelby inquires suspiciously.

"Well, just a little. I can finish it tomorrow morning," replies William.

Exhausted from her day, Mom Shelby imagines that it would be nice to collapse in front of the Brainless herself. But she's too irritated by her children's addiction to television, particularly on school nights. Mom Shelby feels certain that William is avoiding his homework.

If you believe Mom Shelby should say ...

> ... *"I'm just too tired to mess with your homework tonight, William. Take care of it yourself,"* .... **Turn to Scene 130**

> ... *"You have homework, William, and you need to come with me this instant,"* .... **Turn to Scene 134**

> ... *"I'm turning the television off. Everyone find something to read or find something else constructive to do,"* .... **Turn to Scene 129**

SCENE 129

Dad Shelby can't hide his shock: "Turn the television off? But I'm watching the game tonight. It begins in ten minutes."

"Yeah, we're watching the game," chimes in Wally.

"You're not. *I* am," amends Dad Shelby.

"That's not fair," Wally contests. "If you get to watch it, so do I."

"Fair has nothing to do with it, Wally. I'm an adult and I've finished school," declares Dad Shelby.

"But you haven't finished thinking," observes Mom Shelby. "Why don't you tape it and watch it later?"

"You must be kidding. The game won't be over until late tonight. I'll know the score before I could watch," explains an irritated Dad Shelby.

If you believe Mom Shelby should ...

... insist that the television be turned off for everyone, ... **Turn to Scene 143**

*... acknowledge that an exception should be made
    for Dad Shelby,* .... **Turn to Scene 144**

SCENE 130

Mom Shelby decides that she's too exhausted to check William's homework assignments or to fight the spell that the Brainless casts over the Shelby family. Tonight she will surrender and watch television with her family.

No sooner does Mom Shelby understand the plot of *Passion and Violence* than the phone rings.

"It's not for me," Wendy declares, far too comfortable to leave her seat.

Mom Shelby looks around. The Shelby men ignore the ringing phone. Because Mom Shelby displayed concern, the job of answering the phone becomes hers.

Irritated, Mom Shelby walks to the bedroom and answers the phone, "Hello."

"Hello, this is Stephen McKeown's mother," identifies the caller.

Anxiety sweeps over Mom Shelby. Stephen McKeown is the brightest student in William's class. But also, Mrs. McKeown is the volunteer coordinator for the school. Mom Shelby fears that a request for her time is near.

Mrs. McKeown continues, "How is William coming along on the project due in class tomorrow? I hate assignments given three weeks in advance. We always end up doing them the last week. We were wondering if William is including a formal bibliography?" Humiliation might be the most positive emotion Mom Shelby is feeling now.

Mom Shelby is confident that William has forgotten about the project. Worse, Mom Shelby feels incompetent. Stephen McKeown's mother is inquiring about bibliographies while the Shelbys watch a rerun on television.

Mrs. Shelby chooses a safe answer: "No, I'm certain that William has not completed a bibliography and is not planning to submit one at this time. Do you think a bibliography is necessary?"

Mrs. McKeown one-ups Mom Shelby: "Necessary is not the word. A formal bibliography adds quality. By the way, Stephen has been invited to participate in the gifted class next year. Has William heard from the gifted program?"

Mom Shelby's humiliation turns to anger, but she maintains self-control: "No, he hasn't heard. But I believe he'll prefer to stay with his friends if he's asked."

"That's nice. Of course, invitations are already out. But maybe enough people will feel like William and he'll at least have an opportunity to decide. Good luck with your project," Mrs. McKeown replies and then hangs up.

Mom Shelby feels betrayed, incompetent, angry, inferior — how can a three-minute phone call lead her into such emotions?

If you believe that Mom Shelby should say:

... *"William Shelby, come here. We have a lot of work to*
  complete before tomorrow morning," .... **Turn to Scene 137**

... *"William Shelby, come here. You have a lot of work to*
  complete that you neglected to tell me about," .... **Turn to Scene 132**

... *"William Shelby, no more television for you this week,*
  you've left a major project undone," .... **Turn to Scene 131**

SCENE 131

Mom Shelby marches with William to his bedroom. Urged on by her humiliation, she decides to teach William a lesson about responsibility.

"William, how many times have I told you about being responsible for your homework?" asks Mom Shelby. "Stephen McKeown has been working on his project for a week, while you have spent your time watching television. How do you expect to amount to anything if you don't work hard? You're so lazy."

"I don't want to be like Stephen McKeown. He can't do anything but schoolwork," responds William.

"You don't have to be like Stephen to become a good student. You will watch no more television for at least one week. Then I will evaluate how you're progressing. Also, I'm upset that you didn't tell me about your project. William, I'm disappointed. You told me that you could finish your homework in the morning. I'm not sure I can trust you anymore," blasts Mom Shelby.

Quietly, William pulls several sheets of paper out of his backpack. He shows what is obviously a carefully written project to Mom Shelby. Then he walks to his closet and returns with two beautiful pictures of Mars painted on posterboard.

Mom Shelby senses that this may be William's finest work and that she has blundered badly.

"You've been so busy and angry lately, I decided to work on my own. Now, will you stop yelling at me and leave me alone, please?" requests the unrecognized student.

Second Chance! Turn to Scene 130

But first, see **Encouragement** (page 201) and
Encouragement Case Study 3: Keeping Up with the McKeowns
in the *A–Z Parenting Guide* (page 203).

"**W**illiam, you have a lot of homework to do that you didn't mention to me," declares Mom Shelby.

"What homework?" questions William indignantly.

"Mrs. McKeown said Stephen has worked for a week on a project that's been assigned for three weeks. What's the project? You'd better know," threatens Mom Shelby.

"Oh, that project. It's nothing. Just a drawing of one of the planets we've been studying. I already made the picture while I was watching television. Look. I drew Mars on a sheet of notebook paper," explains William.

Mom Shelby looks at a pitiful little ball drawn carelessly in pencil on lined paper.

"William, this is a major project. You can't turn in something sloppy like this. You need to draw Mars on something big like poster paper. Also, you need to use a red marker," Mom Shelby instructs.

"I looked for poster paper. We don't have any. You never have anything in the house I need to do my work," William attacks.

"Why didn't you tell me earlier? I was in the store today," a frustrated Mom Shelby protests.

"O.K., I'll do the project over — just like you suggested. Can you go to the store and get some poster paper for me?" implores William.

If you believe Mom Shelby should say ...

... *"I'll go this once, but this better never happen again,"* ...... **Turn to Scene 133**

... *"I'm not leaving this house again tonight. You'll have to find some other way to do your project,"* .... **Turn to Scene 136**

SCENE 133

"William, I've been working all day and I don't feel like leaving home. But I will this one time, if you promise never to wait until the last minute again," answers Mom Shelby.

"I didn't wait until the last minute. I tried to use poster paper, but you let us run out of it. It's not my fault," William replies.

"O.K., I'll go, William. You stay here and write your report."

Mom Shelby drives to the local drugstore, but it's closed. Fearing that all the stores will be closed, she speeds toward the shopping center. Mom Shelby arrives, parks, and runs toward the department store. The store is about to close and the cashier is not pleased to see a customer slip through the doors.

Mom Shelby pretends that she doesn't care about the surly employee. But for some reason, she does. Nevertheless, she selects the poster paper, purchases it and returns home.

"William, here's your poster paper. I bought an extra piece in case you need it," Mom Shelby announces.

"Great, Mom." William says appreciatively. Then, he adds, "What about the red marker?"

"You didn't ask me to buy a red marker," replies Mom Shelby.

"I told you I needed one and we don't have one. You weren't listening. Now, what am I supposed to do? There must be another store open somewhere," suggests William Shelby.

Mom Shelby slumps, far too exhausted to be able to think about possibilities.

Second Chance! Turn to Scene 146

But first, see **Logical Consequences** (page 217) and
Logical Consequences Case Study 2: Return to Mars
in the *A–Z Parenting Guide* (page 219).

SCENE 134

"William Shelby, I know you have homework. Stephen McKeown's mother told me yesterday that your class has a project on the planets due tomorrow. Come with me," commands Mom Shelby.

William marches behind Mom Shelby to his bedroom.

"Sit at your desk and tell me what your assignment is."

"It's stupid. I don't want to do it. Besides, it's too hard to draw a picture of Mars," William complains.

"Don't be silly. Of course you can draw a picture of Mars. It's just a big red circle," explains Mom Shelby. "We have poster paper. It won't take long."

"I can't draw anything. Wendy's the artist. Can't you help me?" he implores.

If you believe Mom Shelby should say ...

... *"I will help you get started, but then the work will be up to you,"* .... **Turn to Scene 135**

... *"Work on it alone for a while and if you need help later, call me,"* .... **Turn to Scene 138**

SCENE 135

"Find a red marker and a piece of poster paper and we'll start," Mom orders.

"I found the poster paper, but not the markers. Where are they?" screams William from another room.

"Do I have to do everything for you?" Mom Shelby asks.

She walks to William's desk, opens a drawer and pulls out several markers. "They're where you left them. If they had been snakes, they would have bitten you," Mom Shelby says tritely.

"If they were snakes, I could turn them in for my project instead of this dumb drawing," William retorts. "How should I start?" he asks.

"Find a picture of Mars," suggests Mom Shelby.

"Where?" inquires William.

"Is there one in your school book? If not, use the encyclopedias," she replies.

"I left my book at school. Which encyclopedia should I look in?" he asks.

"Do I have to do all of your thinking, William?" Mom Shelby mumbles mechanically. "Look under P for planets or M for Mars."

After a few moments, William yells, "I can't find Mars."

Mom Shelby goes to the den and takes the encyclopedia out of William's hands. In moments she finds Mars and announces, "Here is Mars."

Mom Shelby puts the encyclopedia beside the poster paper and directs William: "Here is the picture of Mars. Take a pencil and draw an outline first. Then you can use the marker."

William picks up his pencil and makes an egg-shaped drawing that covers about one-third of the poster paper.

"William, that's not a circle and it's not big enough," Mom Shelby critiques.

"I can't do it right. Just draw an outline for me, then I'll take over," he begs.

"It's so easy. Just take your pencil and draw a circle like this," instructs Mom Shelby as she draws a nearly perfect circle.

"See, I could never draw a circle as good as yours. This is great. Thanks. I think I'm supposed to draw some clouds on the planet too. Could you draw one of them? You can do it so much neater. I'll copy yours," promises William.

"You really should do this yourself," cautions Mom Shelby. "But I'll draw the first one." Soon the cloud is carefully sketched.

"Mom, which color of red should I use to fill in the planet? Could you get it started for me?" entreats William.

"OK. But this is the last thing I'm going to do for you," vows Mom Shelby.

Second Chance! Turn to Scene 134

But first, see **Encouragement** (page 201) and
Encouragement Case Study 2: My Mars Is Better Than Your Mars
in the *A–Z Parenting Guide* (page 203).

"That's not fair. You have to go to the store. This is a big project. I need poster paper," demands William.

"William, you've known about this project for three weeks. You chose to wait until the night before it's due. You created this crisis and I expect you to solve it," declares Mom Shelby. "Call me if you need me for something else. But I'm not going out of this house."

Mom Shelby leaves the room with mixed feelings. She's never sure how much to help William with his homework. But tonight's emergency seems more a problem of responsibility than ability. Mom Shelby decides to work at her own desk but has difficulty concentrating.

Almost an hour passes and William runs into the study. "Look at my planet! Look at my planet!"

William's face is exuberant as he holds up a large round ball cut out of the side of a box. The ball is painted red and there are puffs of pink clouds made of painted cotton.

"It's beautiful," Mom Shelby proclaims.

"It's my favorite thing I ever did," announces William. "And I didn't even need poster paper or your help."

William's pride seems more gorgeous than Mars. Mom Shelby feels good too. If she had given in to William, he would never have tapped his creativity.

Now, she can turn her attention to new challenges.

Meanwhile, Dad Shelby turns his attention to bath time.

Turn to Scene 148

SCENE 137

"William Shelby, come here. We have a lot of homework to complete before tomorrow morning," commands Mom Shelby.

Unfortunately, the order was overheard by the ever-vigilant Wendy Shelby: "Since when is it *'we* have a lot of homework'? Why do you tell me it's *my* homework, but when William has an assignment, it's *our* homework?"

Dad Shelby looks at Wendy with the pride parents reserve for occasions when children make astute observations. Mom Shelby ignores Wendy's analysis.

"What is this big project about, William?" grills Mom Shelby.

"We're supposed to draw a picture of one of the planets. I'm going to draw Mars because it's just a big red circle with clouds," explains William.

"Let's go to your room and start. We should be finished soon," says Mom Shelby.

Turn to Scene 135

SCENE 138

"All of my children are artistic," Mom Shelby counters. "William, I'm sure you will think of something interesting. Just take your time."

"But, Mom, can't you help?" pleads William.

"Yes, I can. But no, I won't. You can work on it on your own. I'm sure you'll come up with something unique," Mom Shelby encourages.

Mom Shelby leaves William's room and William slams the door. Two minutes later William appears, "Mom, where are the markers and the poster paper?"

"They're either in the den closet or in your room," replies Mom Shelby.

"No, they're not. I've looked there," responds William.

"You didn't take enough time to look thoroughly, William. This sounds like one of those 'Mom-can-find-it-faster searches.' Try again," insists Mom Shelby.

Five minutes later, William appears: "I found the markers and poster paper, but I want to do something special. Give me some ideas, please."

"What have you thought of so far?" Mom Shelby inquires.

"Nothing, I thought I'd ask you first," explains William.

If you believe Mom Shelby should ...

... give William a few ideas to get him started, ... **Turn to Scene 139**

... tell William to think of ideas himself, ... **Turn to Scene 140**

"William, I'll give you some ideas. But you'll have to do the work," offers Mom Shelby.

"That's great!" exclaims William.

"You could take a ball of red yarn and wrap it around one of your small basketballs. That would give a three-dimensional view of Mars," she suggests.

"Come on, Mom. That's dumb. The kids would laugh at it," he complains.

"I'm glad to help, but don't call my ideas dumb," replies an irritated Mom Shelby. "Let's try something else. What if you made a papier mâché ball and used red house paint to paint it? We could dry it in time," she proposes.

"That's stupid! I'd get paint everywhere. Besides I hate papier mâché," gripes William.

"I've had it, William Shelby. I told you not to call my ideas stupid," yells Mom Shelby.

"You did not," counters William.

"I most certainly did. Not more than three minutes ago. Are you hard of hearing?" challenges Mom Shelby.

"No, you just can't remember anything. You told me not to call your ideas dumb. I called your idea stupid. That's different," William explains.

As Mom Shelby leaves William's room, she slams the door and wonders: *How many times will I beat my head against the wall? He always asks for help and then tells me I'm wrong. Who does he think he is?*

Second Chance! Turn to Scene 138

But first, see **Homework** (page 211) and
Homework Case Study 2: You Can Do Better Than That, Mom
in the *A–Z Parenting Guide* (page 213).

SCENE 140

"William, your ideas will be better than mine," exhorts Mom Shelby. "Take your time. Don't rush. You'll think of something."

William slaps a chair in frustration and returns to his room.

This time he stays in his room for several minutes before emerging with a question, "Do we have any string?"

"Yes, dear. It's in the workroom on the counter," says Mom Shelby. William hustles to the workroom and then disappears into his own room.

After twenty minutes, William emerges from his room with a bright smile and his project. Hanging by strings from a coat hanger is a large red kick ball and two little tennis balls representing the two moons of Mars.

"That's amazing!" says Mom Shelby, truly impressed with William's creativity. But she notices that the tennis balls are too big to represent the size of Mars' moons. Ping pong balls would be better.

If you believe Mom Shelby should ...

... suggest how William can improve his work, ... **Turn to Scene 141**

*... applaud William's work as it is and withhold
her observations,* .... **Turn to Scene 142**

SCENE 141

"William, this is terrific. But I think Mars' moons are much smaller than this. Don't you think your project would be more realistic if you used ping pong balls to represent the moons?" Mom Shelby suggests.

William's face changes swiftly from enthusiasm to despair. "You mean my project's not right."

"No. It's great," Mom Shelby assures him. "But your moons are too big. You need to change them."

William drops the project on the sofa and turns away: "I don't want to change them. I can't do anything right."

"You're overreacting, William," assesses Mom Shelby. "Now come back in here and make this simple change. 'Anything worth doing is worth doing well.'"

After hearing Mom Shelby's last pearl of wisdom, William slams the door to his room. Soon the sound of his crying fills the house.

Second Chance! Turn to Scene 140

But first, see **Encouragement** (page 201) and
Encouragement Case Study 1: Who Needs a Critic?
in the *A–Z Parenting Guide* (page 202).

SCENE 142

Mom Shelby decides to hold her tongue: "William, this really is a creative, artistic project. I just love your work."

"Thanks, Mom," William says, still beaming.

"Come in here, everyone, and look at William's project," urges Mom Shelby.

Dad Shelby, Wally and Wendy come to look.

"Wow! That's terrific," Dad Shelby exclaims.

"Neat!" adds Wally.

"What's so great about a bunch of balls hanging from a coat hanger?" William's rival Wendy asks.

But the enthusiasm of the evening outweighs Wendy's obvious jealousy. William feels successful.

"I'm going back to my room," William advises. "I want to make some changes in my project. This is fun."

This hurdle cleared, Dad Shelby turns his attention toward Wally's bath.

Turn to Scene 148

SCENE 143

"I'm sorry about your game, but the television has to be turned off. We must make academics the first priority in the Shelby household," demands Mom Shelby.

"Wait a minute. I don't have homework tonight. I worked hard all day, and I want to watch the game," insists Dad Shelby.

"Think about the model you're presenting to your children. Why don't you read a book about sports?" asks Mom Shelby.

"Who are you to tell me what to think about? Why didn't you think ahead?

You should have talked to me before you came up with this scheme. You don't understand sports well enough to know how big tonight's game is," says Dad Shelby.

"Sports events are never as important as academics," Mom Shelby counters.

Dad Shelby's face reddens and he walks toward the front door. He opens the door and yells, "But maybe good communications are more important than academics or sports. I'll be at Harry's."

Dad Shelby slams the door and drives off.

Second Chance! Turn to Scene 129

But first, see **Values** (page 255) and the
Values Case Study: Ambushed!
in the *A–Z Parenting Guide* (page 256).

"**Y**ou're right. I should have talked to you first," admits Mom Shelby. "But we need to talk privately sometime about television and homework."

"This isn't like watching ordinary television. This is sports. That's different," claims Dad Shelby. "All of you kids get out of here. Go do your homework."

"I don't have any," Wally blurts out. "Can I watch?"

"I guess so," mumbles Dad Shelby, not wanting to precipitate another crisis.

"I'm through, too," adds Wendy. "That means I can watch."

"That's not fair," shouts William. "If they can watch, I can watch. I only have a little bit of homework."

"Finish your work first," demands Dad Shelby.

"Can I do it in here?" inquires William.

"Absolutely not. Work in your room," Mom Shelby says.

William runs to his room and returns in five minutes: "I'm through. I can watch now."

Mom Shelby's temper is boiling. Once again, television has dominated the Shelby household. Then Mom Shelby remembers: "William, isn't your big project on the planets due tomorrow?"

"I just finished it," William answers.

"I'd love to see it, William," Mom Shelby requests.

"My project is on my desk," directs William.

Mom Shelby walks to William's desk and sees a single sheet of notebook paper with the word MARS printed at the top. Below is an egg-shaped red ball with two black dots nearby. At best, William's drawing looks sloppy and incomplete.

Mom Shelby is irate. She charges into the television room and grabs William by the sleeve: "Come with me this instant. Your project is unacceptable."

"No, it's perfect. I did what she said. I drew Mars and its moons," William retorts.

"You rushed through this project so you could watch television. That's wrong, William. You need to do your best work on this project," urges Mom Shelby.

"I need to watch the game with everyone else," argues William.

"Television is killing the children's academics," declares Mom Shelby.

If you believe Mom Shelby should ...

... talk privately to Dad Shelby about the problem, ... **Turn to Scene 145**

... send William back to his room to redo his homework, ... **Turn to Scene 147**

SCENE 145

Mom Shelby approaches Dad Shelby and softly says, "I need to talk with you privately."

Dad Shelby responds well to the soft approach. He follows Mom Shelby into their bedroom.

Mom Shelby begins, "We really have a problem tonight with the television and the children's schedules. William is not doing his work, and the game will run long past the children's bedtimes. I know how important watching this game is to you. Do you have any suggestions?"

She knows that asking Dad Shelby to offer solutions works better than giving him orders. After a moment Dad Shelby suggests, "I don't mind missing the first half of the game, as long as I can see the end. Let's turn off the set and I'll catch the end. That's the most important part anyway."

"Thanks. That's such a help," Mom Shelby whispers as she squeezes Dad Shelby's hand.

Go on to Scene 146

Feeling helpful and in charge, Dad Shelby takes over: "I'm turning off the television. It's time for you to do your homework, William, and for the rest of you to begin getting ready for bed."

"But we want to see the game," Wally pouts.

"Work and sleep are more important," announces Dad Shelby.

"But I need help," declares William. "Mom, I'll do the project over if you promise to help me."

"I'm not promising any such thing, William. What kind of help do you need?" Mom Shelby inquires.

"I guess I should make a bigger picture of Mars. I need poster paper. I can draw Mars with markers," responds William.

"We don't have poster paper, William. Why didn't you tell me earlier? I was in the store today," a frustrated Mom Shelby complains.

"I've got to have poster paper. This is a big project. I didn't know we didn't have any. Can you go to the store and get some for me?" William Shelby asks.

If you believe Mom Shelby should say ;

... *"I'll go this once, but this better never happen again,"* ...... **Turn to Scene 133**

... *"I'm not leaving this house again. You'll have to find some other way to do your project,"* .... **Turn to Scene 136**

SCENE 147

"**G**o to your room right now, William," Mom Shelby directs. "And I don't expect to hear anything from you until your project is done correctly."

William slowly leaves the television room and makes a last request: "Tell me when someone scores."

Mom Shelby sits at her desk catching up on correspondence. She fully expects William to be asking for help within a few seconds. He doesn't.

Mom Shelby hears occasional cheers and jeers from Dad Shelby, Wendy and Wally. There's not a sound coming out of William's room.

Impressed by William's independence, Mom Shelby decides to check in to see how William's project is progressing. She opens William's bedroom door and peeks in. No William.

Mom Shelby senses that her prodigal student must be near the television. She bolts through the living room on the way to the television room. From her vantage point, she can see that William is not with the rest of the Shelbys.

In front of the entrance to the television room, Mom Shelby passes by her antique coffee table. By chance she glances down. Two feet stick out from the end of the table. She stoops down to look.

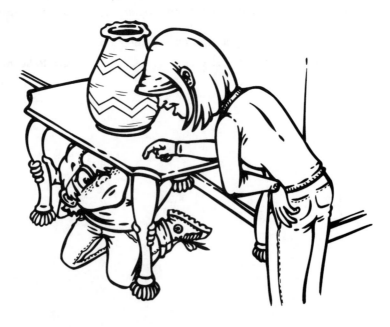

There, mostly hidden from view, is William. No wonder everything had been so quiet. William was watching the game.

Volcanic might not adequately describe Mom Shelby's anger. But no longer is it directed at William. Mom Shelby heads straight to the television and turns it off. Immediately, Dad Shelby roars his disapproval. Another crisis begins.

Second Chance! Turn to Scene 144
But first, see **Homework** (page 211) and
Homework Case Study 1: The Brainless Addiction
in the *A–Z Parenting Guide* (page 212).

SCENE 148

Dad Shelby fills the bathtub with water, thinking, *Tonight I'll spend some special time with Wally. He's had a long day and will be ready for a bath and bedtime.*

Sometimes, Dad Shelby forgets that what's logical for adults isn't as obvious to children.

"Wally, it's bath time. I'll help you," offers Dad Shelby.

"I don't want to take a bath," replies Wally.

"I know, but it's almost your bedtime and you have to take a bath before you go to sleep," urges Dad Shelby.

"Why?" asks Wally.

"Because you're a big boy. Big boys take baths," replies Dad Shelby.

"Not me. I'm not going to take a bath. I'll take one tomorrow," declares Wally.

If you believe Dad Shelby should say ...

... *"You're going to take a bath one way or the other. Do you want to jump into the water or do you want me to put you in?"* .... **Turn to Scene 149**

... *"Let's have a race. I'll turn the timer on for five minutes and see if you can finish your bath before it rings,"* .... **Turn to Scene 160**

... *"Fine. Don't take a bath and we can put plastic sheets down so your bed won't get dirty,"* .... **Turn to Scene 157**

"Wally, do you want to jump into the bath yourself or do you want me to put you in?" inquires Dad Shelby, proud that he's learned to offer choices.

"Neither! I want to play," shouts Wally as he runs from the bathroom.

"This is not what happens in the books," mutters Dad Shelby as he stalks Wally.

Dad Shelby invades the living room. Hiding behind the curtain is Wally. Unfortunately, the curtain covers Wally only from his head to his waist. His legs and feet are totally exposed to Dad Shelby's view.

Do you believe Dad Shelby should ...

... grab Wally and put him in the bathtub, ... **Turn to Scene 150**

... play along with Wally and try to outwit him, ... **Turn to Scene 151**

SCENE 150

"**E**nough is enough," roars Dad Shelby as he grabs Wally from his hiding place. "You had your chance, now I will put you in the tub."

Dad Shelby pulls a twisting, screaming Wally into the bathroom. As Dad Shelby takes off Wally's clothes, the youngster's shrieks almost shatter the windows.

Wally continues to struggle and Dad Shelby remains determined.

"Get in here," shouts Dad Shelby as he lifts Wally to put him in the bath. Wally lands on his feet, standing up in the half-filled bathtub.

"I don't want to take a bath," screams Wally.

"Too bad. Sit down in the water," yells an increasingly agitated Dad Shelby.

"NO. I'm not sitting down and you can't make me," challenges Wally.

"We'll just see about that," retorts Dad Shelby.

As Wally struggles, Dad Shelby reaches into the bathtub and wrestles Wally downward. But as Wally collapses, Dad Shelby loses his balance.

Splash!

Poor Dad Shelby falls head first into the bathtub. Wally's not sure whether to laugh or cry. Dad Shelby is; he bellows.

Second Chance! Turn to Scene 148

But first, see **Games** (page 209) and the
Games Case Study: Dad Shelby Is All Wet
in the *A–Z Parenting Guide* (page 210).

Pretending not to notice the half-hidden Wally, Dad Shelby talks loudly enough for Wally to overhear him.

"I can't find Wally. I've checked the bathtub, so I know he's not there. The bathtub is the one place I'll never look again," promises Dad Shelby.

Dad Shelby purposely clears a path for Wally to reach the bathtub. As he turns his back, Dad Shelby hears the sound of little feet sneaking toward the bathroom. He follows at a distance. With a feeling of self-satisfaction, he hears Wally splash into the water.

Walking into the bathroom, Dad Shelby allows Wally to overhear him: "I just can't find that Wally anywhere. I wonder if he outsmarted me and jumped into the bathtub. No, nobody could be that smart."

When Dad Shelby enters the bathroom, he exclaims with playful surprise: "How did you sneak in here?"

Wally giggles with delight. "I hid from you and you couldn't find me," he chants.

Go on to Scene 152

SCENE 152

Wally plays in the bathtub for several minutes before Dad Shelby announces: "It's time to wash your hair."

Wally's face brightens as he asks, "Can I wash it by myself?"

"We don't have any of the tearless shampoo, Wally. This shampoo can run into your eyes and sting," explains Dad Shelby.

"I can do it, Dad. I'm not a baby. Let me," pleads Wally.

Dad Shelby has seen Wally in action before. His good intentions can be quickly replaced by tears and screaming. After a long day, Dad Shelby isn't ready for a tearful episode. But then again, he's not ready for another confrontation either. One way or the other Dad Shelby feels as if he's about to lose.

"Come on, Dad. Hand me the shampoo. Please!" begs Wally.

If you believe Dad Shelby should ...

... .let Wally wash his own hair, ... **Turn to Scene 154**

... insist on washing Wally's hair, ... **Turn to Scene 153**

"**N**ot tonight, Wally. I'll wash your hair this time and maybe you can do it next time," suggests Dad Shelby.

"No. I want to wash my own hair," pleads Wally.

"Not tonight. Come here and we'll finish the job fast," urges Dad Shelby.

Wally sees that Dad Shelby has no intention of allowing him to wash his own hair. As Dad Shelby reaches for Wally, the youngster "accidentally-on-purpose" knocks the shampoo from Dad Shelby's hand. The shampoo pours out of the bottle and into the water.

"Wally, you've had it," threatens his dad, who is really the one who has had it.

But Wally doesn't wait to discover what *it* is. He vaults from the bathtub to run to his room. But as he rounds the corner, his feet slip on the wet floor and, *BAM!* Wally slams himself onto the floor and begins to shriek: "Mom!"

Tears flow. And when Wally sees Mom Shelby approaching, his howling escalates.

Dad Shelby wants to comfort his son, but is irritated by Wally's appeal to a "higher power" (whichever parent is absent).

Mom Shelby storms in and picks up Wally's crumpled body from the floor, saying, "My poor baby."

Dad Shelby's special moments with Wally have indeed become lasting memories.

Second Chance! Turn to Scene 152

But first, see **Power Struggles** (page 237) and
Power Struggles Case Study 3: Tear-Full Shampoo
in the *A–Z Parenting Guide* (page 239).

SCENE 154

"O.K., Wally, you try it. Be careful. This shampoo can sting," warns Dad Shelby.

"I can do it," Wally brags.

Wally pours shampoo onto his hand and rubs it into his hair. As Dad Shelby walks to the cabinet for a towel, he hears a cry from the bathtub.

Dad Shelby turns to see Wally jumping up and down while rubbing both eyes with his fists.

Dad Shelby runs toward Wally just in time to hear him proclaim: "It's your fault. It's your fault."

After helping Wally rid his eyes of shampoo, should Dad Shelby ...

... set Wally straight by saying: "You have to pay for your
mistakes. You have no one to blame but yourself," ....**Turn to Scene 155**

... say nothing and wait to see what happens,................**Turn to Scene 156**

SCENE 155

After helping Wally free his eyes of shampoo, Dad Shelby decides to set the record straight. But he isn't quick enough. Wally again announces: "It's your fault."

Enraged, Dad Shelby asserts: "It's my fault nothing. I warned you and you insisted on washing your own hair."

Wally persists: "It's your fault. You left me to get a dumb ol' towel. It's your fault."

If there's one thing Dad Shelby can't stand, it's the lack of logical thinking. If there's a second thing he hates, it's blaming others for one's own mistakes. Wally irritates both of Dad Shelby's sore spots with one swat.

"Wally, that doesn't make sense. I was nowhere near you when shampoo ran into your eyes. You did it yourself," Dad Shelby reveals.

"You left. It's your fault," Wally yells. The youngster begins to escalate the crisis by kicking water out of the bathtub.

"Stop that! You're getting water on the floor," shouts Dad Shelby.

"It's your fault. It's your fault," screams Wally.

His last ounce of patience expended, Dad Shelby relies on his remaining good sense: "Mom, come here and take care of your son! He's driving me insane."

Second Chance! Turn to Scene 154

But first, see **Natural Consequences** (page 225) and
Natural Consequences Case Study 5: Pride Precedes Surrender
in the *A–Z Parenting Guide* (page 229).

"It's your fault. It's your fault," insists Wally.

Dad Shelby wants to argue, but he knows not to enter a fight he cannot win. Instead, he helps Wally wash the shampoo out of his eyes.

"It's your fault. You left me to get a towel," accuses Wally.

Dad Shelby says nothing. Instead, he takes Wally out of the bathtub and helps dry him.

"It's your fault. I hate that stupid shampoo. I'm never going to wash my hair again," threatens Wally.

Dad Shelby silently waits out the storm. He helps Wally put on his pajamas.

"It's the stupid shampoo's fault. We have to buy some tearless shampoo next time," pleads Wally.

Dad Shelby knows that he's succeeded. Wally has found something to blame besides his dad or himself. Maybe rationalizing is all right. After all, nothing is as important as an almost-five-year-old's self-confidence.

"You're right. Next time we'll make sure you use tearless shampoo," soothes Dad Shelby.

With that assurance, Wally runs into his bedroom, ready for bed.

Turn to Scene 165

"**F**ine, don't take a bath. We can drape plastic over your sheets so they won't get dirty," explains Dad Shelby, more as a threat than a warning.

"What do you mean drape plastic over my sheets?" inquires Wally.

"When you were two years old, we covered your mattress with plastic to keep it dry when you wet your diapers at night. I can use plastic again — just like when you were a baby. Only now we'll cover the sheets too," explains Dad Shelby.

Dad Shelby studies Wally to see if his explanation creates the desired effect. Wally thinks for a few moment, then declares, "That would be fun. I want plastic over my sheets."

Dad Shelby didn't expect *this* response. In fact, he was certain that his "plastic ploy" would work.

Now what should he do?

If you believe Dad Shelby should ...

... *give up the plastic idea and force Wally to take a bath,* ..... **Turn to Scene 158**

... *put plastic on top of Wally's sheets, as promised,* .... **Turn to Scene 159**

SCENE 158

"**W**ally, I'm not going to look for plastic this late at night. You're not a baby now. Jump into the tub and be a big boy," Dad Shelby urges.

"I don't want a bath and you promised," Wally scolds.

"Wally, I want you in that bathtub this instant," commands Dad Shelby.

"But you promised," whines Wally.

Dad Shelby grabs Wally's arm and pulls him toward the bathtub. As he forces Wally into the water, the furious youngster screams: "You lied to me. You're a liar."

Dad Shelby impulsively drops Wally, then reaches out and slaps his cheek: "Don't you ever call me a liar."

Feeling wronged and hurt, Wally darts out of the bathtub, screaming for Mom Shelby's help.

Dad Shelby sighs. He knows that whatever happens when Mom Shelby arrives will not be pleasant.

Second Chance! Turn to Scene 157

But first, see **Logical Consequences** (page 217) and
Logical Consequences Case Study 3: Empty Threats
in the *A–Z Parenting Guide* (page 220).

Dad Shelby is shocked that Wally wants to cover his sheets with plastic. After swallowing his impulse to retract his offer, Dad Shelby decides to play out his hand.

"I'll put the plastic on while you put on your pajamas," promises Dad Shelby.

Wally prepares for bed and waits for Dad Shelby. Dad Shelby finds the old plastic sheet, but it looks too comfortable. Instead, he chooses a heavy piece of plastic used to protect the furniture during the last house painting job. Dad Shelby brings the plastic into Wally's room.

"That plastic is yucky," Wally complains. "Don't we have any plastic without paint on it?"

"We'll need to use this tonight. But the paint is dry," Dad Shelby explains as he spreads the plastic on top of Wally's sheets. "Hop into bed."

"I don't want to sleep on that yucky plastic," complains Wally to a pleased father.

Dad Shelby decides to press the issue: "Try the plastic. It's not so bad. You may get hot at night, but it beats taking a bath, doesn't it?"

"I want to take a bath," Wally counters.

"It may be too late now. Let me look at my watch," responds Dad Shelby who savors his apparent victory.

"I'll hurry. There's time. I want a bath," begs Wally.

"Well, I'm not sure," Dad Shelby teases. "I guess it will be all right. But hurry up before the water gets cold."

Turn to Scene 152

"I've got a game that no one can win," challenges Dad Shelby.

"Has William ever won it?" questions Wally.

"No. No one can win this game," Dad Shelby answers.

"What's the game?" Wally asks.

"I set a timer for five minutes. You try to finish your bath before the bell rings. But this is a hard game. Maybe we should wait until another night to play it," teases Dad Shelby.

"No! I want to play now. Please. I want to play now," clamors Wally.

Dad Shelby reaches into the towel cabinet and brings out the timer Mom Shelby keeps for such emergencies.

"I'm going to put the timer by the sink where you can see it," explains Dad Shelby.

"Can I put my toys in first?" inquires Wally.

"Sure."

Wally splashes his toys into the water as Dad Shelby sets the timer.

"Okay, Wally. Any time you want to begin, I'll start the clock," confirms Dad Shelby.

"Do 'get ready-set'," requests Wally.

"OK. On your mark. Get ready. Get set. *GO!*" exclaims Dad Shelby as Wally climbs into the bathtub. Dad Shelby leaves the clock eight or nine feet away where Wally can see it. Then he leaves feeling absolutely brilliant.

Looking at his watch, Dad Shelby notices that five minutes have almost passed. He walks toward the bathtub, anticipating that Wally will be ready to spring out.

"It's almost time," yells Dad Shelby as he enters the bathroom.

"No, it's not. I've got lots of time," claims Wally as he points at the timer.

Dad Shelby looks at the timer. Three more minutes are left. Dad Shelby looks at the floor and notices that there are wet Wally tracks to and from the timer.

Obviously, Wally reset the timer. Dad Shelby's game has developed a hitch.

If you believe Dad Shelby should ...

> ... call an end to the game and let Wally know that
> cheating is unacceptable, ... **Turn to Scene 163**

> ... be pleased Wally is taking a bath and sidestep
> Wally's antics, ... **Turn to Scene 161**

SCENE 161

Dad Shelby decides not to challenge Wally about resetting the timer. Nevertheless, he wants to let Wally know that he isn't that easily fooled.

"Seems like your time *should* be up, Wally. That timer surely moves slowly," Dad notes with humor in his voice.

"The timer says I have more time," Wally says.

"Why does the timer think you have more time?" inquires Dad Shelby.

"Because I made it tell me I have more time," explains Wally.

"Do you think that someone should be able to change the timer in our game?" Dad Shelby quizzes.

"You just said I had to get out before the timer rings. You didn't say I couldn't change it," Wally explains.

Wally's comment startles Dad Shelby, creating one of those insightful "Aha!" experiences when parents gain a glimpse of how differently children think.

"I guess you're right. But we need a rule now that no one can change the timer. When it rings in two minutes, you need to get out so we can read," explains Dad Shelby.

"I don't want to get out. I want to play with my toys," Wally counters.

"But you didn't even want to take a bath," blurts Dad Shelby.

"I'm not getting out," declares Wally.

If you believe Dad Shelby should ...

*... say, "Enough is enough. You can't always make up your
    own rules. You must get out of the tub now,"* .... **Turn to Scene 164**

... try to avoid a confrontation and use a game to help, ... **Turn to Scene 162**

SCENE 162

"**Y**ou can't make me get out. I want to play," asserts Wally.

Dad Shelby thinks for a moment and then resorts to a game he's played since William learned the word "NO!"

"I'm going to close my eyes and count to ten and I don't want anyone to get out of that bathtub and dry off," challenges Dad Shelby.

A smile crosses Wally's face. He loves games, particularly when he can surprise his father. Before Dad Shelby reaches six, Wally jumps out of the tub. Dad Shelby continues to count, making sure that Wally is victorious.

Finally, Dad Shelby yells: *"TEN!"*

Opening his eyes, Dad Shelby emits a cry of surprise and joy: "Wally, what are you doing out of the tub? You tricked me!"

Dad Shelby lets Wally know that they're still playing games by his playful tone of voice. "OK. I'm going to close my eyes again and I don't want anyone to put on his pajamas before I count to ten. One . . . two . . . "

Wally rushes to put on his pajamas before the count ends.

Dad Shelby is always amazed how well games work with Wally. True, sometimes Dad Shelby isn't in the mood to play. But when he is, playing games with children usually works better than force.

Turn to Scene 165

"**W**ally, did you get out of the bathtub and reset the timer?" Dad Shelby demands.

"No. It reset by itself," maintains Wally, not comfortable with Dad Shelby's accusatory tone.

"I don't believe you. Why are there wet tracks on the floor? It looks as if you've run back and forth to the timer. That's cheating, and the Shelbys don't put up with cheating," preaches Dad Shelby.

"I didn't do it," Wally yells.

Dad Shelby is always amazed that his children can so easily tell him straight-faced lies.

"Wally, two wrongs don't make a right. *Now* it sounds as if you are lying to me," declares Dad Shelby.

At that moment William, who has overheard the exchange, roams into the bathroom.

"Wally, are you cheating and lying again?" William asks.

Wally feels overwhelmed by his two accusers. He begins to scream.

"Leave me alone. I hate both of you. I don't ever want to play with you again," roars Wally. Fueled by self-righteous anger, Wally runs past William and Dad Shelby in search of more sensitive family members.

Second Chance! Turn to Scene 160

But first, see **Cheating** (page 195) and the
Cheating Case Study: A Federal Case
in the *A–Z Parenting Guide* (page 195).

SCENE 164

"**W**ally, you cannot make your own rules all the time. I've been as patient as I can be — now you need to get out of the bathtub," insists Dad Shelby.

"But I want to play," replies Wally.

"I know you do. But if you want to read, you need to get out now," Dad Shelby advises.

"I don't want to read," blurts Wally.

Dad Shelby realizes that he shouldn't have brought reading into this. Wally always wants to have fun *now*. But he'll be outraged if Dad Shelby refuses to read to him later.

"That's enough arguing, Wally. You need to get out of the bathtub *now*," Dad Shelby says.

"I'm not going to get out!"

Just as Dad Shelby decides to yank Wally out, Wendy runs through the bathroom shouting: "Wally's a jerk. Wally's a jerk."

"Wendy Shelby, go to your room right now. You can't call people names in this house!" exclaims Dad Shelby.

"I hate you, Wendy," Wally screams.

"Wally, stay out of this. I'll handle Wendy while you get out of the tub and put your pajamas on. I'll meet you at your bed," says Dad Shelby.

Wally can't resist seeing Wendy in trouble. He jumps out of the bathtub as Dad Shelby walks toward Wendy's room. Dad Shelby normally would be perturbed with Wendy. Tonight, he's not. By accident, her misbehavior put Wally and Dad Shelby on the same team.

What would have happened if Wendy hadn't come in? Dad Shelby muses. For once something bad turned out well.

Turn to Scene 165

SCENE 165

Finally Wally's bath is over. In a rare moment of quiet, Dad Shelby thinks about his long day.

What have I done for myself today? he thinks. Of course, Dad Shelby never asks himself this unless the answer is "little or nothing." Maybe later he can spend a few minutes in his workroom or catch the end of the ball game. Time will be scarce, however, because Wally always reads before he goes to sleep. By habit, Dad Shelby glances at his watch.

"Wally, it's late. In fact, it's your bedtime," Dad Shelby announces, with the hope that he can sneak away early to his workroom. "We won't have time to read tonight."

"We have to read," demands Wally. "We always read."

"Maybe not tonight, Wally," explains Dad. "I have some things I need to do and it's getting late."

"Please, Dad. I want to read," begs Wally.

If you believe Dad Shelby should ...

... do something for himself and skip reading because
it's late anyway, ... **Turn to Scene 181**

... find something different and exciting to do
that will take less time, ... **Turn to Scene 184**

... stick to Wally's routine, ... **Turn to Scene 166**

Wally insists on reading. Finally, Dad Shelby decides it would be easier to read than to disrupt Wally's bedtime routine. But, he hopes, Wally will read something new.

"Okay, Wally. Let's read. But let's read something different tonight. Here's a book we've never read before," observes Dad Shelby as he picks out an adventure book.

"But I want to read *Green Eggs and Ham*," protests Wally.

"Wally, you've read that a million times. We both know it word for word. Let's read something new," suggests Dad Shelby.

"I love *Green Eggs and Ham*. Please, Dad," begs Wally. Dad Shelby is still annoyed that he's missing his ball game. Now, it looks as if he'll also have to read again a book that he's read countless times.

If you believe Dad Shelby should ...

... read Wally's favorite book, ... **Turn to Scene 169**

... insist that Wally try a new book, ... **Turn to Scene 167**

"I'll read to you under one condition: that we try this new book," Dad Shelby says.

"Let me see it first," requests Wally.

Dad Shelby brings the adventure story to Wally's bed and lies down beside him.

"This story is still one of William's favorites," Dad Shelby tells Wally.

"Then I don't like it," Wally decides. "Besides, it doesn't have good pictures."

Dad Shelby leafs through the book and realizes that Wally is right. The book doesn't have many pictures and is rather complicated. But it's different!

It may be a little difficult for Wally, Dad Shelby thinks. *But he'll catch on.*

"Let's give it a try, Wally. Just this once," pleads Dad Shelby.

"Okay. But if it's boring, can we read my book?" petitions Wally.

"Sure. But you're going to love this book," Dad Shelby assures.

Dad Shelby begins to read the adventure story. Wally tries to follow, but after the first sentence he interrupts: "Dad, what's a musket?"

"It's a type of old rifle," explains Dad Shelby, then he reads on.

Two sentences later Wally interrupts again, "Who was Blackbeard?"

"He was a pirate," Dad Shelby explains and continues.

A few seconds later Wally stops Dad Shelby: "I don't know what's going on. Tell me."

"Blackbeard has kidnapped this little boy. But the boy escaped with a musket and is trying to find his way home," summarizes Dad Shelby.

"This is boring. Can we read *Green Eggs and Ham?*" Wally requests.

If you believe Dad Shelby should ...

... read Wally's book, ... **Turn to Scene 169**

... explain that it will take time to understand the new book
and read on, ... **Turn to Scene 168**

SCENE 168

"**W**ally, you need to be patient. You'll understand the book if you listen carefully. This is a terrific story," says Dad Shelby.

"I hate this story," Wally answers.

"We've begun this book and we need to finish it, Wally. Besides, I like adventure stories. You'll like it, just wait," urges Dad Shelby, before he resumes reading.

After two or three minutes, Wally can tolerate no more. He knocks the book out of Dad Shelby's hands and yells, "I hate this book!"

Dad Shelby is enraged that Wally slapped the volume away: "We don't treat books like this in our family. You just go to bed without reading."

Dad Shelby springs out of Wally's bed, snatches the book off of the floor and storms out of the room.

Wally howls, but Dad Shelby couldn't care less.

"That boy is so unappreciative," Dad Shelby fumes. "Reading to him is awful. What a brat."

Second Chance! Turn to Scene 167

But first, see **Respect for Self and Others** (page 242) and
Respect for Self and Others Case Study 2: My Way or No Way
in the *A–Z Parenting Guide* (page 243) .

SCENE 169

At least *Green Eggs and Ham* is relatively short, considers Dad Shelby as he begins to read. And reading surely beats fighting.

Dad Shelby has finished the first few pages when he hears the phone ring. In a few moments William yells, "Dad, it's for you."

"Who is it?" asks Dad Shelby.

William comes in the room with his answer: "I don't know. It's some man who asked for Mr. Shelby."

"I'm almost through reading," Dad Shelby says to William, as if William would help him decide whether or not to talk. But William says nothing and Dad Shelby must make the decision.

If you believe Dad Shelby should ...

> ... *talk briefly on the phone, and hope that Wally goes to sleep while he's gone,* ....**Turn to Scene 170**

> ... *ask William to take the name and number so he can return the call,* ....**Turn to Scene 171**

SCENE 170

While *I'm gone maybe Wally will go to sleep. Besides, this may be an important call,* Dad Shelby reflects.

He walks to the kitchen and picks up the receiver. "Hello."

The voice on the other end begins, "Is this Mr. Shelby?"

"Yes, it is."

"Hello, I'm collecting money for the Taboo Recovery Fund. We're a non-profit organization that provides support to families who have broken the taboos of their culture and are needlessly persecuted . . ." recites the fund raiser.

Dad Shelby isn't sure whether to listen to the entire monologue or to interrupt the caller. He decides to be polite, even if the fund raiser isn't.

Finally, the caller ends with, "Mr. Shelby I know you want to support us. Can I put you down for $100, $50 or $25?"

Dad Shelby responds: "I'll need to talk this over with my wife. Send some literature and we'll make a decision."

"What if I put you down for $25? Then if you and your wife want to give more, that would be greatly appreciated," presses the caller.

"No, we need to talk first," explains Dad Shelby.

"Would you be able to talk tonight? I can call later," pushes the fund raiser.

"I don't think we can tonight, but soon," replies an irritated Dad Shelby.

"Why don't I put you down for $25 and send you the information," insists the anonymous voice.

"NO! I have to go. Good night," Dad Shelby shouts.

By the end of the phone call these guys make you believe that you owe them money and are welshing on a debt, thinks Dad Shelby as he walks toward Wally's room.

At least Wally may be asleep, hopes Dad Shelby as he peeks into Wally's room.

WRONG!

Far from asleep, Wally is on the floor surrounded by his stuffed animals. He appears to be playing "Animal Trainer," a game he invented after visiting the circus.

Wally looks at Dad Shelby with disdain: "Get out of here. You're disturbing the wild animals. Besides, they might kill you."

With that warning, Wally slams the door.

Second Chance! Turn to Scene 169
But first, see **Routines** (page 246) and
Routines Case Study 3: Called from Routine
in the *A–Z Parenting Guide* (page 248).

SCENE 171

"William, please take the man's number and tell him I will return his call in a few minutes," instructs Dad Shelby.

"Where were we?" asks Dad Shelby. Finding his place in the book, he resumes.

Fatigue strikes. To lie down is to go to sleep when you're a parent of young children.

First Dad Shelby feels drowsy. His eyelids become heavy and he struggles to keep reading. Then he slurs his words. Once or twice the book drops from his hands.

"Wake up, Dad!" Wally implores.

Dad Shelby awakens, but slowly his eyelids grow heavier. He stops reading.

Wally looks at his father. The exhausted man is asleep with his mouth hanging open and Wally's book resting on his chest. Wally crawls over Dad Shelby and leaves the room.

"Come look!" Wally urges Wendy.

Wally's tone of voice promises Wendy that her trip will be worthwhile. When she sees Dad Shelby, Wendy whispers, "Go get William."

Soon the three Shelby children stand over Dad Shelby. Wendy hushes her brothers and with a gleam in her eye discloses: "I have a plan."

The Shelby brothers follow Wendy into their parents' bedroom. Wendy searches through Mom Shelby's closet for the appropriate clothes, then hustles back to Wally's bedroom.

In a matter of seconds, Wendy drapes Mom Shelby's dress over Dad Shelby and places a fancy hat on Dad Shelby's head.

William runs back to Mom Shelby's room and returns with a pocketbook and some jewelry. Hoping to record this event for the Shelby album, Wendy locates the family camera. Finally, Wally brings Mom Shelby to the crime scene.

As Mom Shelby enters, she bursts into laughter. There sleeps Dad Shelby, adorned in Mom Shelby's best Sunday clothes. Dad Shelby is a deep sleeper, but Mom Shelby's laughter instantly awakens him.

Dad Shelby looks confused at first. But he soon catches on and joins in the laughter. The camera flashes and another chapter of Shelby family folklore is born.

"I think you need some rest. I'll take over," offers Mom Shelby. "Come on, Wally. It's time to sleep. William and Wendy, it's time for you to go to bed as well."

After Mom Shelby's announcement, everyone scatters.

"It's nice to end the day on a fun note," observes Mom Shelby to Wally. But Wally is too busy searching his room to hear.

"Wendy took my binky," Wally accuses.

Instantly Mom Shelby knows the seriousness of the situation. Wally's binky is the baby blanket bound with a satin ribbon that accompanies him to sleep each night. Whenever Wally's upset, his binky calms him. He loves to rub the soft lining against his face.

"Are you sure Wendy took it?" asks Mom Shelby, although she suspects that Wendy did. Whenever Wendy pulls one prank, she usually thinks of several others.

"She took it! She took it!" exclaims a frantic Wally.

"Calm down, Wally. You and I've been talking about your giving up the binky. You know you can't carry it around forever," Mom Shelby says gently.

"I have to have it tonight," insists Wally.

"Why?" inquires Mom Shelby.

"I just do," explains Wally.

If you believe Mom Shelby should ...

*... take advantage of the situation and wean Wally
from his binky,* ....**Turn to Scene 172**

... retrieve the binky and fight the binky-battle another day, .. **Turn to Scene 173**

SCENE 172

Mom Shelby decides to take advantage of the situation and to help wean Wally from his blanket.

"Wally, tonight would be a good time to give up your binky. You're a big boy now and you won't be able to take your blanket to school next year," explains Mom Shelby.

"I have to have my binky. Wendy stole it. Please get it from her," Wally entreats.

"Not tonight, Wally. Just calm down and I'll rub your back," offers Mom Shelby.

"I need binky. I have to have binky," Wally pleads, becoming more adamant.

Mom Shelby holds Wally and gives him a hug, "Come on, Wally. Let's try to do without your blanket tonight."

Fueled by his exhaustion from the day, Wally pitches a "Wally Tantrum." Stomping his feet and screaming, Wally pushes Mom Shelby away.

With the timing of an accomplished antagonist, Wendy appears in the doorway with Wally's blanket.

"Is this what you want?" she asks.

"Yes," says Wally, reaching for his treasure.

"Can't have it!" yells Wendy who runs away with Wally's binky under her arm.

Wally is enraged, and his fit takes on monstrous dimensions.

Mom Shelby looks on — in total defeat.

Second Chance! Turn to Scene 171

But first, see **Routines** (page 246) and
Routines Case Study 2: The Stolen Binky Caper
in the *A–Z Parenting Guide* (page 247).

Mom Shelby decides not to spring the binky-removal project on Wally without warning.

"I'll find your blanket. You jump into bed," Mom Shelby directs.

Mom Shelby walks into Wendy's room in a manner that suggests the youngster must cooperate or *else*.

"Wendy, enough is enough. Give me Wally's blanket this instant," commands Mom Shelby.

Wendy doesn't want to tangle with Mom Shelby. After all, she's still enjoying her successful episode of dressing up Dad Shelby. She doesn't want to ruin the evening just to tease her little brother.

"Here it is, Mom. I don't know how his binky got in my room. He probably left it here." Wendy knows that Mom Shelby doesn't believe her. Nevertheless, she enjoys supplying an alibi to match every accusation.

Mom Shelby returns to Wally's room.

"Here's your binky. Now, are you ready to say your prayers?" asks Mom Shelby, more as an order than a question.

Wally affirms his readiness and begins: "Bless all of the people in the world who don't have as much as we do. Bless Mom and Dad . . . and William . . . and Wizard . . . and please let Wendy live on another planet. Amen."

"Wally, be nice to your sister," Mom Shelby admonishes, suppressing her laughter.

"I hate her," Wally declares.

"Think how that would make Wendy feel. Besides Wendy will be your best playmate tomorrow, I bet," Mom Shelby assures a skeptical Wally.

"She will not," Wally declares. Having said the last word, Wally snuggles deeply into his covers. He clutches his binky and kisses Mom Shelby goodnight.

"I love you," Mom Shelby affirms.

"I love you," replies Wally.

Mom gives Wally a kiss and begins to walk away.

"Mom, I need a drink of water," requests Wally.

Mom Shelby doesn't reply, but fills a glass with water and returns. Wally takes a sip and nestles back under the covers as Mom Shelby leaves the room.

"Mom, I'm hungry," Wally calls out.

"I'm sorry. It's too late to eat anything," Mom Shelby responds.

"Mom, tell Dad to come in so I can give him a goodnight hug," Wally requests.

"I'm sorry, Wally. Dad's busy. I'll tell him goodnight for you," promises Mom Shelby as she tries to leave again.

"Mom, I'm not tired. Can we sing?" asks Wally.

Mom Shelby is clearly irritated: "No. Just go to sleep, Wally." She quickly leaves the room and begins to read in the den.

No more than a minute passes before Wally walks into the room dragging his blanket behind him.

"Mom, I can't sleep. Will you sit with me for a minute?"

If you believe Mom Shelby should ...

... *agree to sit in the room until Wally goes to sleep,* .... **Turn to Scene 175**

... *pick Wally up and take him back to his room and
leave him on his own,* .... **Turn to Scene 174**

... *take Wally back to his room and agree to check on him
in a few minutes,* .... **Turn to Scene 176**

Mom Shelby carries Wally back to his bed and tucks him in again.

"This will be the last time I tuck you in, Wally. If you leave bed again, I will just carry you back. Our time is over. I'm not talking with you any more. This is my time now," explains Mom Shelby.

Mom Shelby returns to her reading chair and resumes reading. Before she finishes the first page, Wally runs into the room and announces, "I'm not tired."

Without saying a word, Mom Shelby picks Wally up, carries him to bed and gently places him on top of his covers.

When she leaves, Wally cries for her. Mom Shelby doesn't respond and returns to her reading.

After reading five pages, Mom Shelby hears Wally creeping toward her chair. Quietly, she leaves her chair, picks him up and deposits him in his bed. Despite his protests, Mom Shelby returns to her reading chair.

This scenario repeats itself three more times. Each time Mom Shelby returns silently to her reading chair.

Mom Shelby reads a few more pages before Wally sneaks toward her once again. She calmly rises and takes a stride toward him. Knowing that he will once again be unceremoniously dumped in his bed, he runs back to bed on his own.

Mom Shelby resumes reading. If tested on anything she read, Mom Shelby knows she would fail.

"It may require a week or so to train Wally," Mom Shelby reflects. "But from now on when it's time for him to sleep, I'm not going to play games and reward him with extra attention."

Finally, Wally is quiet and Mom Shelby feels pleased. She finishes the easy job of saying good night to William and Wendy. Both of them are independent at night — at least most of the time. But when they were younger, they had played the same games that Wally enjoys.

Mom Shelby closes her book and listens to how quiet the house has become. The day has been long and challenging. Nothing sounds better than the sound of her quiet home.

Turn to Scene 177

SCENE 175

"I'll sit with you for a few minutes," replies Mom Shelby.

Mom Shelby walks toward a rocking chair in the corner of Wally's room. The chair has rocked her through many long nights of children's earaches, stomach aches and croup. Tonight it seems like an old friend.

With the lights out, Mom Shelby begins to rock. The sound of the squeaky chair rockers soothes Wally. The rhythmic creaking calms Mom Shelby as well.

"Maybe sitting with Wally is not the best habit to have," Mom Shelby muses. "I guess it would be better to leave. But do I ever enjoy these moments when no one would dare bother me. These are the times when I can think or do nothing at all."

Mom Shelby isn't sure if Wally is asleep. She drifts into her own thoughts so intensely that time seems lost. For a moment, she drifts into that state between awareness and sleep.

Finally, she is awakened by Wizard the cat rubbing against her leg. Mom Shelby walks to Wally's bed.

"What an angel," she thinks.

With a feeling of peace, she walks toward the den. "Finally, a few moments to read," she thinks.

Turn to Scene 177

"Wally, this is my reading time," begins Mom Shelby. "If you stay in bed, I will come back and check on you in a few minutes."

"Thanks, Mom," Wally says contentedly.

Mom Shelby sits down and reads three pages. Then she returns to Wally's room. He's awake, looking out for her.

"Mom, can we make up a story?" begs Wally.

"No, but I will check on you again in a few minutes if you stay quiet," Mom Shelby assures.

She fluffs Wally's covers around his shoulder, then resumes her reading. After six pages, she returns to Wally's room. This time, Wally is drowsy.

"I love you," Wally mumbles.

"I love you, too," Mom Shelby replies.

Mom Shelby pats Wally's back and returns to her reading. Twelve pages later she checks on Wally. This time he's asleep. She watches him.

"Sometimes," she thinks, "I feel as if I might like to have ten more children. It's a good thing I can remember all of the day's events or I might lose perspective."

With a chuckle, Mom Shelby returns to her reading. By this time William and Wendy are preparing for bed. They'll drift off to sleep on their own later.

The house seems still and peaceful. Mom Shelby knows no better sound at night than quiet. The day is almost over.

Turn to Scene 177

SCENE 177

Dad Shelby joins Mom Shelby. Fortunately, tonight William and Wendy put themselves to bed with little assistance from their parents. Sometimes it seems that the Shelby children take turns resisting sleep.

Dad Shelby whispers, even though the children are out of earshot. "This quiet is marvelous," he confides, "I don't want it to end."

Mom Shelby pats her husband's hand. "I know. These peaceful moments seem miraculous. We just didn't appreciate what we had before we had children, did we?" she muses.

"I guess not, but most of the time these kids seem worth it," confesses Dad Shelby with a twinkle that shows his devotion to his children.

These special moments don't present themselves frequently in a house filled with children. Mom and Dad Shelby relish every second.

Abruptly, the silence ends. "Help! Help! Mom! Dad! Help!" a voice shrieks.

Disoriented for a moment, Mom and Dad Shelby look at each other, trying to determine whose voice they hear.

"Wally!" they shout simultaneously. The alarmed parents sprint to Wally's room and discover him weeping hysterically.

"A monster was in my room trying to get me. It ate Wendy and was chasing me. I hid under my bed and the monster was looking for me," Wally rambles.

"You had a nightmare, Wally," Mom Shelby calmly explains. "You're O.K. now. We're here and there is no monster."

"Yes, there is a monster. I know he's here," asserts the terrified four-year-old.

Wally Shelby grabs his mother's hand: "Let me sleep with you tonight. Please. Let me sleep with you and Dad."

If you believe the Shelby parents should ...

    ... tell Wally that everything is fine and that he should
      go back to sleep, ...**Turn to Scene 178**

    ... have Dad Shelby look everywhere in Wally's room
      and scare away all the monsters, then lock the windows, ...**Turn to Scene 179**

    ... have Mom Shelby offer to allow Wally to sleep
      in their bed for the night, ...**Turn to Scene 180**

SCENE 178

"**W**ally, you had a bad dream. But it was just a dream. Everything is fine," Mom Shelby assures Wally again.

"Mom, there are monsters. I saw them," responds Wally.

"Don't be silly, Wally. Monsters are pretend," Dad Shelby adds.

"I'm scared. Please let me spend the night in your room," Wally pleads.

"No way, Wally," Dad Shelby asserts. "You need to handle these scares on your own without our help. You will face scary things throughout your life. You must stand up to them. You'll be fine. We're leaving now."

Mom Shelby, less than sure that Dad Shelby's approach fits, kisses Wally good night and tucks him in again. "I love you," Mom Shelby assures Wally.

The Shelbys return to the den. Mom Shelby picks up her book and pretends to read. But she worries about Wally. Dad Shelby is irritated that their special moment was interrupted. He also senses that Mom Shelby believes he was too tough on Wally. Time passes, but there are no more sounds from Wally's room.

Mom Shelby resists her desire to check on Wally for a long time. Finally, she tiptoes toward Wally's room, but she doesn't need to go far. On the floor at the entrance to the den lies a sleeping Wally Shelby. He's curled up in a fetal position, clutching his binky and favorite stuffed bear.

Mom Shelby's insides feel hollow. Suddenly she feels as if she's the most uncaring parent in the world — with one exception.

"How could you!" murmurs Mom Shelby to her husband.

Mom Shelby gently carries him back to his room. Now Dad Shelby feels not only like a callous dad, but also like an unappreciated husband.

Second Chance! Turn to Scene 177

But first, see **Fears** (page 207) and the **Fears Case Study: Monsters in the Night** in the *A–Z Parenting Guide* (page 207).

Dad Shelby interrupts, "I'll take care of this, Wally."

The heroic Dad grabs one of Wally's toy swords and waves it through the air. "If there are any monsters here, they'll be gone in a second. They're terrified of your magic sword."

Dad Shelby goes through the room, looking in all of Wally's drawers and under the bed.

Wally joins the game and yells, "Out of here, monsters."

Dad Shelby laughs, "That did it, Wally. You've scared every monster in the world away."

Dad Shelby closes Wally's window and announces: "Now, no monsters can get back into your room."

"Yeah," agrees Wally. "We really got them, didn't we?"

"We sure did," confirms Dad Shelby. "Mom Shelby and I will be in the den reading, if you need us. We'll keep the door cracked."

Wally smiles at Mom and Dad Shelby.

"We sure showed those monsters," Wally brags.

"You surely did," adds Mom Shelby.

Mom Shelby tucks Wally in again, kisses him and leaves with Dad Shelby.

The two sit in the den and listen. But no more sounds come from the little warrior's room. Soon he drifts to sleep, exhausted after winning a battle over the monsters in his life.

Turn to Scene 189

"I guess you can sleep with us tonight," Mom Shelby agrees reluctantly.

Dad Shelby's shock is apparent: "Sweetheart, can we talk outside for a minute?"

"Sure," Mom Shelby agrees. "Wally, we'll be right outside your door."

They leave the door partly open. Wally seems satisfied that they are near.

Dad Shelby begins, "We *just* got Wally out of our bed. We don't want him to sleep with us every time something scares him. Having him sleep with us for so long caused us lots of problems."

"I know, dear," concedes Mom Shelby. "But he's so little. And I know that he's really scared."

"I agree. But it's a mistake to teach him he can't handle his problems in his own bedroom. Isn't there something you can do to help without starting a bad habit again?" asks Dad Shelby.

"You're right. It's harder to get Wally out of our bed than never letting him into it. But I can't just leave him here," explains Mom Shelby.

"Isn't there some middle road?" pleads Dad Shelby.

"Okay, I'll think of something," replies Mom Shelby, as she returns to Wally's room.

"Wally, the monsters were just a dream. But I'll give you a back rub. Then I'm going to read in the den, just a few feet away. I'll check on you every few minutes before I go to bed."

Mom Shelby kneels beside Wally's bed and rubs his back. Dad Shelby returns to the den. After a few minutes, Mom Shelby joins him.

"Is he asleep?" Dad Shelby inquires.

"Not quite, but he's close," replies Mom Shelby.

She sits for a few minutes, then checks on Wally. He looks up at her and smiles. Mom Shelby leaves. Knowing that she will check on him again, Wally feels free to slip into sleep.

The Shelbys remain in the den until they're certain that Wally is asleep. Then they walk to Wally's bed and marvel at him.

Wally is asleep, clutching his binky. His stuffed bear stands guard over him. With his parents' help, Wally has conquered the dragons of the night.

Turn to Scene 189

SCENE 181

"We don't have time to read tonight, Wally. I have lots of things I need to do. Besides it's late and you need your sleep," declares Dad.

"But Dad," pleads Wally.

"No buts. Tonight I just have too much to do. Now, hop into bed and I'll cover you," Dad commands.

Wally follows his dad's orders. The youngster is angry, but he knows it won't do any good to protest. Instead, he'll play along and save his complaints.

Dad Shelby mechanically tucks Wally in and says goodnight.

Free at last, Dad Shelby goes to the kitchen to make a snack.

Mom Shelby asks, "Is Wally in bed?"

"Sure," replies Dad Shelby. "No problem. He's exhausted."

No sooner does Dad Shelby's appraisal leave his tongue than Wally strolls into the kitchen.

"I can't sleep. Will you read a short book to me?" Wally requests.

If you believe Dad Shelby should ...

... *stick to his guns and refuse,* .... **Turn to Scene 182**

... *return Wally to his nightly routine and read to him,* .... **Turn to Scene 183**

SCENE 182

Dad Shelby quickly replies before Mom Shelby can.

"Wally, I told you there would be no reading tonight and that's the way it's going to be," Dad Shelby affirms.

With Mom Shelby near, Wally takes a chance: "Why?"

"Because I said so and I'm your dad," replies Dad Shelby. "Go to bed. Now!"

Wally looks toward Mom Shelby for help. She's caught between supporting her husband and helping Wally. Finally, convinced that Dad Shelby is wrong, Mom Shelby enters the fray.

"Let's compromise. Wally, I'll read a few poems to you. That won't take long," Mom Shelby risks.

"No reading! I said no reading and I mean no reading!" shouts Dad Shelby.

"But, Sweetheart," Mom Shelby begins. But Dad Shelby feels too humiliated by her overrule to listen.

"Do what you want to do. You're turning Wally into a spoiled brat," roars Dad Shelby. An instant later, he slams the kitchen door and marches toward his workroom.

Second Chance! Turn to Scene 181

But first, see **Routines** (page 246) and
Routines Case Study 1: Takes a Brat to Know a Brat
in the *A–Z Parenting Guide* (page 246).

SCENE 183

Mom Shelby responds quickly, "Sweetheart, maybe reading a short book would help Wally go to sleep. I can do it if you want to work."

Dad Shelby realizes that he took a shortcut that threw Wally out of his routine. If he leaves now, he'll feel guilty. After all, Mom Shelby had a rough day too, and reading to Wally was his job tonight.

But Dad Shelby knows that Wally will want to read *Green Eggs and Ham* again. They've read it two nights in a row and Dad Shelby wants a change.

"Okay. We'll read, but we need to make a deal."

Turn to Scene 167

SCENE 184

"Let's do something different tonight, Wally. We read every night," Dad Shelby complains.

"What are we going to do?" quizzes Wally.

"Let's sneak in the kitchen and eat a snack," suggests Dad Shelby.

"A snack! Great!" Wally clamors.

The two hustle into the kitchen, trying to avoid detection by Mom Shelby. They know she doesn't approve of bedtime snacks. In the kitchen, Dad Shelby takes some chocolate chip cookies out of a cabinet and pours a soft drink for each of them.

"You have to promise to go straight to bed after our snack, Wally," Dad Shelby demands.

"It's a deal," Wally vows.

The two gobble several cookies and guzzle their soft drinks.

"Now let's sneak back to your room," advises Dad Shelby.

Back in bed, Wally whispers, "That was fun!"

Dad Shelby feels wonderful. He reaches down and tickles Wally. The youngster howls with excitement.

Hearing Wally's squeals, Mom Shelby walks into the room.

"What's going on?" Mom Shelby asks.

"Nothing!" Wally and Dad Shelby simultaneously reply.

One look at the chocolate on Wally's mouth tells Mom Shelby everything she needs to know. She leaves the room. Dad Shelby winks at Wally and follows her into the den.

A few moments pass and Wally strolls into the den.

"I can't sleep. Can we read?" Wally requests.

If you believe Dad Shelby should ...

... hold Wally to the deal they made, ... **Turn to Scene 185**

... read to Wally to avoid a confrontation with Mom Shelby, ... **Turn to Scene 186**

"**W**ally, we made a deal. You have to hold up your end of the deal. Be fair," declares Dad Shelby.

"Fair!" exclaims Mom Shelby. "*You* excited Wally. *You* calm him down."

"I didn't do anything wrong. We had a little snack, that's all," claims Dad Shelby.

"You shot sugar into his system. Now, you want him to sleep. Who's being unfair?" Mom Shelby asks rhetorically.

"Wally, get to bed," demands a besieged Dad Shelby.

"I'm having nothing to do with this," declares Mom Shelby. Looking Dad Shelby directly in the eye, she orders: "You take care of this child. You know better than to excite him before bedtime."

With her declaration made, Mom Shelby stalks out of the room.

Second Chance! Turn to Scene 165
But first, see **Routines** (page 246) and
Routines Case Study 4: Sugar-Charged Bedtime
in the *A–Z Parenting Guide* (page 248).

Dad Shelby knows he'd better take charge of Wally or face the wrath of Mom Shelby.

"OK, Wally. Let's read a short book," Dad Shelby offers.

"Let's read *Green Eggs and Ham,*" suggests Wally.

Dad Shelby groans. Better to do it, though, than to contend with an irate Mom Shelby.

"Sure, let's read it," concedes Dad Shelby.

After reading the book, Wally announces: "I'm not tired. Can you lie down with me?"

Dad Shelby knows that he's made a mistake. Mom Shelby has told him countless times not to excite the children at bedtime. To abandon Wally now would lead to an inevitable quarrel.

"Sure. I'll lie down with you, but just for a few minutes," agrees Dad Shelby.

After turning off the lights, Dad Shelby lies down with Wally. A few minutes later, he tries to escape.

"Where are you going?" questions Wally.

"I need to get some work done. Settle down and go to sleep," Dad Shelby urges.

"I can't sleep. I'm wide awake. Let's sing," entreats Wally.

Dad Shelby feels totally outsmarted. If he leaves, Wally will have a "Wally Tantrum." If he stays, his evening will be lost.

Second Chance! Turn to Scene 165

But first, see **Routines** (page 246) and
Routines Case Study 4: Sugar-Charged Bedtime
in the *A–Z Parenting Guide* (page 248) .

"I know that everyone needs to help with chores," explains Dad Shelby. "But I put in a long day at the office and sometimes I don't feel as if it's fair to come home and have to do more work."

"You do work hard, dear. What you're saying is that you don't feel we appreciate your hard work?" Mom Shelby asks.

Dad Shelby looks surprised, "I didn't realize it, but *yes*. That's exactly what I mean."

"I understand," Mom Shelby explains. "That's exactly how I feel many times."

"Me too," blurts William.

"You. What do you mean?" asks Mom Shelby.

"I work all day in school and when I come home you or Dad always tell me to do this and do that," explains William. "I want time to play."

As Mom and Dad Shelby listen to William, Wendy jumps into Dad Shelby's lap and gives him a hug, "We appreciate you, Dad. We all love you, particularly *me*."

Dad Shelby rarely cries, and he's determined not to now. But his eyes water as he says, "Thanks Wendy. I guess I just need to hear that from everyone once in a while. I love each of you, too."

The rest of the Shelby clan is silent. Dad Shelby has never made a public declaration of love before. For a moment, the family is unaware of time, as if this moment will endure forever.

Finally Dad Shelby suggests, "Why don't we finish choosing chores, and we'll talk about jobs again in a few days."

Everyone nods approval.

Dad Shelby looks at Mom Shelby. "How would you like to wash dishes with me tonight? We need some time alone."

"I'd love nothing better," Mom Shelby says.

Turn to Scene 128

SCENE 188

Dad Shelby intervenes. "What have you kids done now?"

The Shelby children look in fear at Dad Shelby's imposing figure.

"Your son has stolen candy from my store," the clerk testifies.

"Wally Shelby, give the candy back," demands Dad Shelby.

Wally hands the crumpled candy bars to the clerk.

"Sir, we don't want these candy bars back. He needs to pay for them," explains the clerk.

The clerk's tone irritates Dad Shelby, "You stay out of this and let me talk to my son."

Now the clerk is provoked with Dad Shelby.

But Dad Shelby continues, "Wally pay the man."

"I don't have enough money," Wally whines.

Dad Shelby reaches in his pocket and realizes he left his wallet at home, "Who has enough money to pay?"

"Don't look at me. I'm not paying," Wendy declares.

"Me either," says William.

"Someone has to pay," snaps the clerk.

"Let *us* handle this," Dad Shelby replies.

"You don't seem to be able to handle it," the clerk replies.

Dad Shelby turns red and demands, "Take us to the manager."

"Gladly," responds the clerk.

Second Chance! Turn to Scene 68

But first, see **Stealing** (page 251) and the
Stealing Case Study: Caught Chocolate-handed
in the *A–Z Parenting Guide* (page 251).

It's late, as always, when Mom and Dad Shelby retire.

"Tomorrow comes too soon," Dad Shelby hints with a gleam in his eye. "I'll take a quick shower, then can you hurry yours?"

Mom Shelby understands that even after their long day Dad Shelby feels a bit frisky.

Dad Shelby rushes to bed and Mom Shelby hurries in her deliberate way. Finally finished with her nightly routine, Mom Shelby crawls into bed and snuggles close to Dad Shelby.

Mom Shelby peers into the darkness and reflects aloud, "You know, our kids can be a handful, but I wouldn't trade them for the world."

After a pause she continues: "But we'll have time to think of them later. Now, you were saying something about needing to delay going to sleep . . . maybe with a little excitement?"

Mom Shelby turns toward Dad Shelby — just in time to see his mouth fall open and to hear one of the most thunderous snores in Shelby bedroom history.

Mom Shelby watches her husband breathe. Dad Shelby is still the best-looking man she has ever seen. Then again, even the Shelby children seem perfect when asleep.

CONGRATULATIONS!
You Survived an Ordinary Day
With the Shelbys

(Sleep well. The alarm sounds again at 6:15 in the morning.)

Dear Readers,

Thanks! The Shelbys needed help, and you did an incredible job of helping them make tough choices. Raising children may be the most difficult challenge we face in life. Because of you, the Shelbys will be better prepared to meet the challenges of William, Wendy and Wally — at least, I hope they will be. Practice makes perfect!

Oh, my, what's that sound? It's the Shelbys' alarm clock. Another day is about to start. I wonder how it will go.

Stay tuned for future Shelby adventures!

My best to each of you,

Dr. Ken West

The Shelbys'

A–Z Parenting Guide

Complete with Case Studies

Introduction

"**A** second chance! When I was in school, I dreamed of retaking tests — particularly after I knew the questions," chirps Dad Shelby.

"Me, too! And as a parent, I've wished hundreds of times that I could go back and change my mistakes. Now, with the help of our readers, we'll enjoy second chances," says Mom Shelby.

Dad Shelby adds, "We asked our friend Ken West to help, too. In this *A to Z Parenting Guide*, he discusses more than forty ideas that work in raising children. But the longest distance in the world is between theory and its application to the Shelby children. That's where Mom Shelby and I come in."

Mom Shelby advises, "After the reader reviews a theory, we'll apply the idea to the specific problems we confronted in the main story. After you hit a "Second Chance," flip to the theory and case study suggested. We'll do our best to offer helpful hints. After you read our discussion, return to the main story and help us make another choice. Through your decisions, we'll enjoy a second chance. William, Wally and Wendy will appreciate your help, but not as much as Dad Shelby and I will!"

Dad Shelby explains, "You'll notice that the ideas Ken West presents begin to weave together. Therefore, we'll highlight (with **boldface** type) additional themes you may wish to read before returning to the main text."

Mom Shelby concludes, "Dad Shelby and I may not always agree, but we'll work hard to make your decisions easier. Thanks for taking the time to help us. Oh — and when you return to the story, you'll once again find *The Shelbys Need Help!*"

A

Attention-getting Behaviors

All children need attention. Hugs, kisses, and compliments should be plentiful in any home. Children learn early that they can gain attention through both positive actions and misbehavior.

When attention-getting becomes misbehavior, parents feel annoyed. An attention seeker demands to be the center of the parent's attention at inappropriate times (for example, when the parent is talking on the phone), or in improper ways. Although many attention-getting behaviors are clearly misbehaviors, children also may demand attention by trying to be "better" than others. Wendy does that (see Scene 72) by being a tattletale.

Although attention-getting misbehaviors are common to all children, parents need to prevent children from becoming addicted to a need for constant attention. Attention addicts can grow up to be adults who always need the approval of others to feel worthwhile and loved.

Tips for parents:

- If you feel annoyed by a child, you may be dealing with attention-getting misbehavior.

- When possible, ignore misbehaving attention-getters and avoid making eye contact with them.

- Give attention to children on your terms, not when it is inappropriately demanded.

- Catch children being good and offer your **encouragement** regularly and liberally when children behave well.

The Shelbys:

"I guess adults use attention-getting antics, too. Look at Uncle William; he always has to be the center of attention. Every time the family tries to have a serious conversation, he makes bird calls and buffalo noises," observes Dad Shelby.

"That's true. But I'm more concerned about Wendy. I knew listening to her tattling wasn't right, but I couldn't figure out why her behavior annoyed me so much. Now I

know," *Mom Shelby says, as a battle breaks out in the next room.*

"Oh, no! William and Wally are fighting again. Why do they always seem to fight when we're busy?" Dad Shelby wonders.

"Attention-getting! They just forced us to stop our conversation and become busy with them. Let's be less predictable this time and ..."

B

Bribery

Bribes may offer parents temporary victory, but in the long run they usually lead to trouble. Bribes backfire most severely when they are given as rewards for activities that should be part of a child's ordinary responsibilities. Why should a child be rewarded for dressing, finishing chores, or studying? Such behaviors should be expected.

At worst, children who are bribed begin to work only when a reward is offered. After they become accustomed to a reward, children tend to go on strike until parents offer more and more. Giving rewards is like stumbling into quicksand. After you resort to bribes, it becomes increasingly difficult to escape the trap. Take my advice: Avoid the quicksand! Use **encouragement** and **logical and natural consequences** instead.

BRIBERY CASE STUDY: Dressing for Snacks

"Wow! I made my first mistake when I bribed Wally to do something that he should do anyway," confesses Mom Shelby.

"But you were rushing. You thought a bribe would hurry things along," Dad Shelby consoles.

"That's true. But after I made the mistake of bribing Wally, things became worse and worse. I felt as if I were sliding on ice. I could see what was happening, but I couldn't stop myself."

*"Then came the famous Wally **temper tantrum**. Bribes almost always lead to tantrums — eventually," Dad Shelby points out.*

"Yes, and I was such a sucker that I played into his hands. I whacked Wally and he, of course, escalated the fight into World War III. I wish I could go back and resist my first temptation to use bribes."

"You can't do that, but the reader can take you back to the scene of the "Wally Tantrum." Do you have any advice?" asks Dad Shelby.

*"Indeed I do! Get off the ice. Don't let the situation escalate. Take Wally out of the store. He may kick and cry all the way, but at least by removing him I will show **respect for myself and others.** No one else should have to endure Wally's tantrums,"* Mom Shelby replies.

"You're right. That bribe initiated a bad chain of events. With the reader's help, you can put an end to it right now."

Second Chance: Turn to Scene 32

C

Cheating

We want our children to play by the rules. If parents provide family **values**, children will eventually follow their example. However, children are not adults. They do not think as we do. Cheating by adults and teenagers is a far more serious offense than it is for young children.

Preschool children possess wonderful imaginations (see **intelligence, lying** and **stealing**). When they play games, they see no problem changing the rules as they go along. Parents who attempt to force children to think like adults usually provoke pointless **power struggles.** Also, they lose out on the enjoyment of a child's unique world of thought. Eventually, most elementary school-aged children begin to follow the rules. But even then, they may develop their own rule: *I cannot lose or fail.*

Parents need to make their expectations known. At the same time, they must respect a child's limitations. Children's thinking is simply not as advanced as adults'. Model your values. Be patient. Avoid overreacting.

CHEATING CASE STUDY: A Federal Case!

"I guess I sucked the air out of that good time," admits Dad Shelby.

"You were tired, dear. When we are tired, we're not always flexible," Mom Shelby says.

"True. Still, Wally was just playing. And there were no rules for the game. I just assumed ..." begins Dad Shelby.

"Assumed that Wally would think just like you do?" asks Mom Shelby.

"Exactly. I acted as if all games had to follow adult logic. Next time I will realize that when I enter a child's world of play, I need to be more flexible. There's no way to forecast how a game will end until you reach the conclusion."

"Right. Wally didn't cheat. He just wanted to have fun and didn't want to be bothered by an adult's need for law and order," concurs Mom Shelby.

CHORES

*"It's a long way from the Supreme Court to a child's bathtub," observes Dad Shelby.
"At least you can wash your hands of this ending and begin again."*

Second Chance: Turn to Scene 160

Chores

Performing chores allows children to feel that they are important members of the family. Outside of rural settings, many parents may find it easier to do everything themselves. But that attitude robs children of a feeling of being valuable.

Preschool children profit from performing a few simple tasks. They need constant **encouragement** as they learn how to be helpful. As children grow older, they should be expected to contribute more.

Variation helps. Some families draw jobs from job jars. Others provide a list at **family meetings** and allow each member to take turns selecting chores. If children fail to perform their jobs, use **logical and natural consequences** and discuss the problem at the next family meeting. Avoid giving rewards as a **bribe** for doing routine chores and accepting necessary responsibilities. Feeling like a contributing member of the family is reward enough.

CHORES CASE STUDY: Forks to the Left!

"Only the cook knows how frustrating it is when no one will lift a finger to help!" asserts Mom Shelby.

*"You're right. But it was not just Wally, we all failed you. We need a plan so that whoever cooks isn't forced to do all of the work. Maybe a **family meeting** devoted to chores would allow us to create a schedule for the week," Dad Shelby suggests.*

"Nothing could help more. But what should I have done when Wally wasn't doing the job correctly?"

*"You're the one who usually advises that we do things together. You and Wally were both resentful. Maybe if you had **communicated** your feelings better, then Wally would have worked with you to solve the problem."*

"That sounds reasonable. But I was really frustrated. It's difficult to be reasonable and angry at the same time," confesses Mom Shelby.

"You were feeling hurt and hopeless. But if you had known that we would create a schedule for chores in the near future, you would have been hopeful."

"You're right. I needed the assurance that the future would improve. If I could just go back, I would work better with Wally. Then we could solve the main problem later as a family," Mom Shelby concludes.

"Yes, when major problems like chore distribution aren't solved, then small problems appear to be gigantic."

Second Chance: Turn to Scene 123

Communications

"I will talk. You listen." That seems to be what some people consider to be communications. For them, a poor communicator is someone who does not do what is commanded. To the contrary, good communications involve being both a good listener and a careful speaker. Below I will share ideas that have been helpful to my family.

Ideas that Enrich Communications

- When you listen, try to capture the main ideas and feelings of speakers. Reflect back on the points people are making and the feelings they share to let them know you understand.

- When you speak, share your feelings and be exact about the things you need to have happen. Do not assume people can read your mind; they cannot. Be specific.

- When angry, hurt, or upset, use "I statements" instead of "you statements." Others are more likely to listen when we take responsibility for our feelings than when they feel blamed or when we call them names. For example, "I feel hurt when you leave me out of your weekend plans" will work better than "You make me so angry when you act like a self-centered wildebeest."

- Be assertive. Avoid passivity and aggression. Passive people become doormats for others. They fail to let people know their feelings, thoughts, and needs. On the other hand, aggressive people get what they want but hurt others unnecessarily. Hot warriors harm people with their temper tantrums, shouting, and intimidation. Cold warriors punish others into submission by giving them the cold shoulder and silent treatment.

- Communicate your happiness and appreciation for others as assertively as you do your dissatisfactions. Children need to know what they are doing right even more than they need to know what they are doing wrong.

- Take time for communications. **Family meetings** provide a wonderful opportunity for everyone to talk and listen.

COMMUNICATIONS

The Shelbys:

"Is he kidding? Ken West said that these were ideas that proved to be helpful to his family. Do you think professionals use their own ideas?" Mom Shelby asks.

"I suppose they must. After all, our author has three kids — just like we do. He has to do something when they drive him crazy," responds Dad Shelby.

"Drive him crazy. He's a family therapist. I doubt his kids ever misbehave," Mom Shelby maintains.

"Are you serious? How do you think Ken West lost most of his hair!" quips Dad Shelby.

COMMUNICATIONS CASE STUDY 1: Cold Warrior Attacks

"If I admit that I am a hot warrior, will you admit that you are a cold warrior? One is just as bad as the other," offers Dad Shelby.

"How can being silent be as bad as yelling at someone? I feel absolutely devastated when you scream at me. Not only do you wipe me out, but also we never talk about our problems," counters Mom Shelby.

"I admit that yelling when I'm angry makes the situation worse. Granddad Shelby was like a volcano. He let steam build up over time, then he'd explode at the first person who crossed him. I'm afraid I never had a model who shared feelings in a constructive way. But I'm willing to try new ideas."

"When I was young, my parents never allowed family members to show anger. In fact, I can still remember Mom telling me how ugly I looked when I lost my temper. Eventually, I began to stuff my anger. Maybe I began to hide any feeling that wasn't pretty," explains Mom Shelby.

"You don't exactly stuff feelings. I know you are angry at me when you refuse to talk and give me the cold shoulder for days at a time. How do you think that makes me feel?" Dad Shelby probes.

"I don't know exactly. How does it make you feel?"

"I feel absolutely devastated. In fact, I feel wiped out just like you do when I scream. And we never really talk about problems. Instead, I walk on eggshells and try anything to bring you back into the relationship," Dad Shelby explains.

"I feel pretty rotten right now."

"I don't want you to feel rotten. And I don't want to devastate you or be destroyed any longer. Instead, let's be honest and open with each other. Where shall we begin?" asks Dad Shelby.

"It would help if the reader would give us another chance. This time I'll be up front with my feelings."

Second Chance: Turn to Scene 120

COMMUNICATIONS CASE STUDY 2: You Do the Dirty Work

"I knew that refusing to clean the bathroom was a mistake. But I felt cornered, and I suppose I became defensive," explains Dad Shelby.

"You mean you weren't really refusing to do the chores?" Mom Shelby asks.

"Well, I didn't want to clean the bathroom, but if there had been time to think about things I would have agreed. My first reaction was to say no. But before I could think about it, I felt attacked," admits Dad Shelby.

"I believe I understand. You were feeling a loss of control. Then when I came on too strong, you felt humiliated."

"Yes. You're right. I was fighting for control, and I didn't really care that much about chores," admits Dad Shelby.

"I suppose I was disturbed more about feeling unappreciated and undervalued," Mom Shelby adds.

"In other words, our fight had nothing to do with cleaning the bathroom. I was fighting over control issues, and you were battling for respect for yourself and others," Dad Shelby concludes.

"That's ironic. Neither of us understood what the other was saying. We were both stuck in our own worlds. I wish we had just asked, `What is this disagreement really about?'"

"Exactly. If only we could go back in time. I would react differently," imagines Dad Shelby.
"Maybe we can ..."

Second Chance: Turn to Scene 113

Contingencies (Grandmom's Law)

"When you finish your dinner, then you can eat your ice cream," Grandmom would say. She knew that children need to complete less desirable activities before they enjoy more desirable ones. On the other hand, Grandmom would never say, "Eat your ice cream, then you can enjoy your spinach." Always make the more desirable activity contingent upon completing the less enjoyable task.

The Shelbys:

"No wonder William didn't clean up his room," Dad Shelby says.

"What do you mean?" asks Mom Shelby.

"I told him I would let him go outside and play if he promised to clean up his room as soon as he returned," explains Dad Shelby.

"Aha! You broke Grandmom's Law. What did William do when he came in from playing?"

"First, he turned on the television. Then second, he set my temper on fire. Next time the 'ice cream' comes last," Dad Shelby chuckles.

D

Dressing

Young children (2 and 3) undress better than they dress. When they are in a "terrible twos" mood, dressing them can lead to Armageddon. When parents feel hurried, they tend to plunge into **power struggles.** Frequently, indirect methods work better.

Keys to More Peaceful Dressing

- Give children choices: "Do you want to wear your blue shirt or your yellow shirt?" (Hope they do not reply, "Neither.")

- Older preschoolers can usually select their own clothes. Their selections may not match. Use **encouragement** and save your "coordinated colors" lecture for a teachable moment.

- Walk away from resistant children: "When you are ready to dress, find me." This technique works best when you enter the bathroom and close the door behind you.

- Play **games,** such as, "I bet I can dress before you do." (Be sure to lose!)

- Avoid giving **bribes** to children or they will refuse to dress until you make your best offer.

- If power struggles escalate, use **logical consequences:** "We will leave in five minutes. If you are not dressed, you can go to preschool in your pajamas or dress in the car."

"I don't need to be told I made a mistake when Wally refused to dress. This is one power struggle I dove into head first without checking the water," admits Mom Shelby.

"We've both been there, and we've both hit bottom. We're so rushed in the morning that it's easy to use force when other methods work better," Dad Shelby says.

*"You cannot imagine how scared I was. Hitting Wally was wrong. Then when he wet his pants deliberately, I met his act of revenge with a childish response of my own. Physical punishment not only doesn't work well, but it can also be dangerous. Instead of shaking Wally, I should have backed off and thought of a **logical consequence.***"

"Don't be so hard on yourself. We are all learning as parents. You're a wonderful mom or you wouldn't be trying to find new ways to handle trying situations," Dad Shelby consoles.

"You've made me feel better. I just hope the reader will give me an opportunity to use a superior training technique."

Second Chance: Turn to Scene 31

E

Encouragement (The Magic Technique)

No attitude proves to be more crucial in changing negative atmospheres and in building self-esteem than an encouraging one. Encouragement builds positive relationships with children, spouses, friends and co-workers. Encouragement is almost magical — the "rain that makes children grow."

Courage is crucial to successful living. When we criticize children and focus on their disabilities, we discourage (dis-courage) them. They begin to lose their courage, confidence, and enthusiasm.

Critical parents indirectly teach their children that they are never good enough. As a result, youngsters may quit trying or become perfectionistic in an attempt to be beyond criticism.

Encouragement reflects a specific attitude about life rather than a set of techniques. People who encourage well are like cheerleaders. They dwell on the positive and believe people are on the verge of success rather than approaching failure. Children need encouragement most when they try something novel or difficult. Always look for the positive, even if you can only applaud the effort. Resist the temptation to criticize youngsters when they need support. At a later time, when children are ready to listen, help them learn new or improved ways of handling difficult tasks and situations.

ENCOURAGEMENT

If you have any doubt about the power of encouragement, make four consecutive positive statements to someone you love. Observe and enjoy the change in your relationship. Just hope your positive comments don't shock your loved one!

ENCOURAGEMENT CASE STUDY 1: Who Needs a Critic?

"I still think that William was being overly sensitive. I told him that I loved his project. All I did was offer a simple suggestion. Why did he have to take my observation as criticism?" asks Mom Shelby.

"It probably wasn't what you said as much as your timing. William wasn't ready to hear your suggestions. Do you remember the time you took the art course in water colors?" asks Dad Shelby.

"I sure do. What a wonderful experience! Well, almost wonderful ..." recalls Mom Shelby.

"Exactly. You painted a picture of our house with the children playing in the background. I bet you know where I'm headed."

"I know. When I finally found the courage to show you my masterpiece, you mentioned that the children seemed too large."

"And do you remember how you reacted?" leads Dad Shelby.

"Exactly like William did. I ran into my room and sobbed. I felt so hurt that after all of my effort you found a mistake," responds Mom Shelby.

"I learned from my faux pas. Whenever people try something new, they're sensitive. We need to wait until they're ready to hear suggestions, or they will be devastated by our criticism," counsels Dad Shelby.

"I tend to rush in with critiques because I tend to be perfectionistic. When I dream of **utopia***, it's easy for the children to think their efforts are never good enough," Mom Shelby answers.*

"I agree."

"In this case I was right, but I needed to hold onto my advice until William was ready to listen. I was a classic not-good-enougher."

"Life is strange. It's not what we know, or even being right, that counts. What is crucial is timing and technique. We need to sense when children are ready to listen to our suggestions," Dad Shelby reflects.

"Yes, children are just like us. Sometimes we need support and not another critic."

Second Chance: Turn to Scene 140

ENCOURAGEMENT CASE STUDY 2: My Mars is Better Than Your Mars

"I know that I shouldn't help William this much with his homework, but he's so helpless," Mom Shelby notes.

"William's so helpless because you're so helpful," Dad Shelby reflects.

"He is helpless because I am helpful? That doesn't make sense."

"When you provide better ideas, William depends more and more on you to think for him and to complete his work. He's beginning to lose confidence in his own ability because your ideas always seem superior. William is discouraged. He is literally losing the courage and confidence to work on his own," explains Dad Shelby.

"But he doesn't have any ideas. He just sits there and waits for someone to help."

"Let him sit. He'll think of something when he realizes we won't think for him."

"But his ideas aren't always good," responds Mom Shelby.

"**Utopia** is not the goal. Learning to think for himself is. A mediocre idea that William originates is better than a wonderful notion that you create," reasons Dad Shelby.

"But I'm worried about his grades. He needs help to make good grades," reflects Mom Shelby.

"He needs help to become independent. He's a good student. But he's becoming dependent on you. You passed the third grade; now William needs to," reasons Dad Shelby.

"You mean I should never help?" snaps Mom Shelby.

"You should help him when he truly needs help, rather than when YOU lose confidence in him."

"I'm not sure I agree. I'll always wonder what would have happened if I had just left him alone," puzzles Mom Shelby.

"Maybe you won't need to wonder long. Our readers will probably help."

Second Chance: Turn to Scene 134

ENCOURAGEMENT CASE STUDY 3: Keeping Up with the McKeowns

"I feel terrible. When Mrs. McKeown bragged about her son's work, she hooked into my competitiveness. I just wanted to take a swing at her," Mom Shelby admits humorously.

"Even if you swung with William's fist," quips Dad Shelby.

"Yes, my reaction was my problem, not William's. I know that I showed a lack of confidence in William by assuming that he had not completed his work. But I don't think my mistake was devastating."

"Far from it. In fact, William felt as if he had really taught you a lesson."

"William did teach me. I need to show confidence in my children. But most of all, I need to look before I leap," concludes Mom Shelby.

"You're right. Children tend to live up to our expectations. When we show our confidence, they usually act competently," replies Dad Shelby.

"Yes, and sometimes they act competently even when we act childishly. Take that Mrs. McKeown. William is doing just fine — thank you. Next time my personal doubts creep in, I'm going to show my confidence in my family."

"Maybe your next time will come sooner than you think — with a little help from our friends."

Second Chance: Turn to Scene 130

Experts

You are the expert when it comes to your own children. Listen to professionals. But remember: No one knows your children as well as you do. Follow your intuition. Always be an advocate for your children during difficult times.

The Shelbys:

"Wow! That's what I needed to hear," says Dad Shelby.

"Me, too. Sometimes listening to so much expert advice from so many people makes it difficult to decide what to do."

"Aunt Williford won't make the most obvious decision without calling the pediatrician six or seven times. I bet she drives that poor doctor nuts," observes Dad Shelby.

"You've got that right. Besides, in the end the big decisions are always ours to make. We should never totally rely on professionals to make decisions for us. We need to do what we tell our children to do: Think for ourselves," observes Mom Shelby.

"A brilliant deduction, my dear!"

F

Family Meetings

No single activity can contribute more to a marriage and family than family meetings. It is essential for modern, busy families to share a specific time each week when family members can plan fun events, discuss challenges, and prepare for the coming week.

Before they can actively take part in meetings, toddlers benefit from seeing their parents discuss issues peacefully. Soon, young children themselves can pound the gavel and call a meeting to order. Later, they can participate in short meetings that feature a time to plan family fun. Eventually, children become full participants by voting and discussing family problems. Participation in family decisions offers youngsters assurance that they are important and understood.

Although family meetings conform to the specific needs and preferences of individual families, they usually include common elements.

Secrets to Successful Family Meetings

- Meetings should be held regularly.

- All family members should attend. If anyone misses a meeting, then he or she must abide by the agreements made until the next meeting.

- Rotate the chair and secretary positions each week.

- Do not nag spouses or children during the week. Except in emergencies, save discussions for the family meeting.

- Parts of the meeting can include sharing appreciations, distributing **chores**, discussing problems, and planning family fun.

- Votes should be taken only when parents can live with the results. Do not vote on whether or not Dad should quit his job and move to Australia, for instance.

- Meetings are not always easy. Parents need patience. The benefits of working together far outweigh the headaches.

FAMILY MEETINGS CASE STUDY: Flight of the Neanderthal

"Don't think for one moment that you can return to the Shelbys-as-usual. Not only did you reject family meetings, but also you were a bully. I cannot believe your **communications**. *I will not allow you to dictate rules, tell us to obey, and then walk out of the house,"* declares Mom Shelby.

"I needed time to think. I've cooled off now," replies Dad Shelby.

"Well, I have NOT. We have worked together to move this family toward more open communications and increased cooperation. Suddenly, you balk and become more authoritarian. I feel abandoned and discouraged," complains Mom Shelby.

"Suddenly may be the right word. I was not prepared for such a big change. Why didn't you talk with me first? I felt ambushed by you and Wendy."

"Ambushed? I thought that family meetings made so much sense that you would immediately appreciate the idea."

"You thought wrong. After all, I came from an authoritarian home. I've made big changes in my behavior already. Family meetings scare me," explains Dad Shelby.

"You're right; you've always tried to make important changes. That's why I thought that the meetings would appeal to you. I admit I came on too strong. Maybe we should have talked first. Nevertheless, family meetings are important to Wendy and to me," insists Mom Shelby.

"I know. But isn't there a middle ground? Can't we start slowly?"

"Okay. How would you like to begin with a couple's meeting? You and I will sit down together to discuss family meetings. I'll explain why they're important to me and how they can improve our family," offers Mom Shelby.

"As long as I can share my ideas and feelings, I have no objections. In fact, I think a couple's meeting would be a good idea. There are other issues we need to consider," adds Dad Shelby.

"I'm sure you will eventually like the idea of meetings. And I'm willing to discuss things that are important to you, too," Mom Shelby replies.

"How about after supper?"

"Fine. I like this addition already. At least we're scheduling important discussions rather than avoiding them."

Second Chance: Turn to Scene 112

Family Therapy

When an adult encounters trouble with a golf swing or a financial decision, he doesn't hesitate to ask for the help of a coach or advisor. Families are more complicated than a fairway slice or a new investment. When any member of a family faces difficult challenges, parents will profit from psychological coaching.

Family therapists understand that problems may stem from interactions parents may not notice. Also, when an entire family attends sessions, everyone can offer support and become a part of common solutions.

FAMILY THERAPY CASE STUDY: Hopeless in Center City

"I know you're writing this book, but I needed someone to talk with ... and, you know. Well, of course, you know that Dad Shelby and I are fighting, and I didn't have the courage to ask the counselor to call me back," explains Mom Shelby.

"I understand. I'm pleased we're talking," responds Ken West.

"Do you think going to a counselor is a sign of weakness? Maybe I should handle these problems by myself," wonders Mom Shelby.

"Attending counseling displays your wisdom and strength. A weak person might wallow in misery or not care enough about herself or others to seek help," explains Dr. West.

"But I really believe I should be able to handle my problems."

"You are handling your problems by contacting the counselor. Therapists won't give you the perfect answers, but they will help you sort through your feelings, examine your possibilities, and choose a plan of action."

"I hear what you're saying. In the end, I'll make the important decisions. I will be the one who decides on a plan to make life better."

"Exactly. Counselors help, but they cannot return to your family and make changes. You will do all of the work," adds Ken West.

"I'm ready to call. In fact, I feel better already."

"I'm not surprised. Making an appointment is frequently the biggest leap one can take toward healthier living," Dr. West observes.

Second Chance: Turn to Scene 117

Fears

Developing fears of certain objects, creatures and situations is a normal part of childhood. Babies have an innate fear of loud noises and falling. Other fears arrive at predictable ages. At about eight months, toddlers become frightened of strangers. Most fears, such as fear of strangers, leave as predictably as they came. Time is the surest cure.

Around the age of two, children's imaginations dramatically increase. Between the age of two and five, children's bedtime fears include intruders such as ghosts, animals, or monsters. Nightmares increase because the imagination is growing. Parents need to offer children assurance. Also, adults can frequently drive away imaginary bedroom villains and lock the windows behind them. An imagination that initiates fears can also calm them.

Although some fears are healthy (fear of speeding cars, for example), others require intervention. Explanation, time, and gradual experience help children overcome many common fears, such as fear of dogs or water. However, when fears become extreme enough to interfere with daily life, children may need the help of a counselor.

FEARS CASE STUDY: Monsters in the Night

"I don't know whether I'm more angry with your insensitivity to Wally's fears or with me for going along with you," storms Mom Shelby.

"My insensitivity! Wally needs to face his fears," Dad Shelby explains.

"Yes, but he doesn't need to face them alone. Not when he's almost five," snaps Mom Shelby.

"But his fears aren't real. There are no monsters in his bedroom."

"His fears are real to him. Maybe you can explain to Wally why you hate to fly and won't climb onto the roof. After all, you have an irrational fear of heights," Mom Shelby says.

"No, I have a fear of falling. Come to think of it, I have a fear of hitting the ground!" laughs Dad Shelby.

"This isn't a laughing matter. When you fly, you have help," claims Mom Shelby.

"I do not. I fly alone when I need to."

"If you don't have help, what do you call taking a ton of sedatives or gulping a bunch of cocktails?" asks Mom Shelby.

"Okay. You're right. But I didn't mean to be insensitive. I just wanted more time with you," mumbles Dad Shelby.

"Well, you succeeded. We've just spent time arguing about the fears of a four-year-old. Next time, I'm going to be more sensitive. I know I can scare those monsters out of Wally's room."

"That's the truth! You just scared me into submission!"

Second Chance: Turn to Scene 177

Fighting

Parents will never eliminate fighting from their homes. Instead, they should create rules to handle these inevitable altercations and squabbles.

Young children need to learn to solve their own disagreements, although they would prefer that adults intervene for them. When a disagreement is brought to a parent, a consistent response should show respect for the children's abilities to solve their own interpersonal challenges: "I am sure you can handle this on your own." Also, parents can direct children to take their fights outside or downstairs. Fighting usually ends when an audience is not near.

If fights escalate and parents must become involved, specific rules help: "Anyone who hurts another goes to **quality time out** automatically," or "If I must intervene in a fight, then everyone involved goes to time out." Although one child frequently is blamed for a fight, usually all are participants. Equal treatment usually works better than trying to figure out who is "most" guilty.

The Shelbys:

"Poor William," sighs Mom Shelby.

"What do you mean?" asks Dad Shelby.

"Because William is the oldest, he always gets blamed for fights. Wally and Wendy know just what buttons to push to drive him crazy," Mom Shelby responds.

"Yeah. They know how to drive you wild, too. From now on I'm going to send them all to their rooms until they cool down."

"Not me. I'm going to tell them to settle it themselves."

"I don't think that will work as well. You need to send them to their rooms," says Dad Shelby.

"Don't tell me what to do! If they would learn to settle problems themselves, we wouldn't need to be involved in the first place. You should make them work things out," Mom Shelby snaps.

"Why don't we just ask Ken West which one of us is right?" Dad Shelby suggests.

"Forget it. He'll just tell us to figure it out on our own."

G

Games

Discipline does not always require seriousness. Take advantage of a child's love for games. When children resist, do the unexpected: play. For instance, the obstinacy of the "terrible twos" can usually be handled with "reverse" psychology: "I am going to close my eyes, and I don't want anyone to sneak into the bathtub," or "Let's race to see who can dress first."

Children play games for fun. Too frequently, competitive parents lose their perspective when playing with children. **Cheating**, for instance, usually suggests that the child has lost interest in the parents' rules. Parents would be wise to reduce competition and focus on enjoyment and teamwork. For example, instead of playing basketball against your son or daughter, play together against an imaginary team. Each time your team makes a basket, your team scores. When you miss, the other team scores. Adjust the rules to make games fun.

GAMES CASE STUDY: Dad Shelby Is All Wet

*"Don't give me a speech about **power struggles**. Wally needed a bath. I simply was not in a mood to play games," Dad Shelby attacks.*

"I suppose you were in the mood to snorkel," quips Mom Shelby.

"That's not funny. Sometimes Wally must do what I tell him to do — immediately."

"You're acting like an architect again! Bridges and buildings work according to plan. Children don't. They think. They have emotions. They defy your blueprints. You must work WITH children," says Mom Shelby.

"It's so frustrating. Things are so easy at the office. Children are unreasonable," retorts Dad Shelby.

*"Their **intelligence** is different. You're right. But it's easier to work with them than against them. Sidestepping struggles for power will save you lots of pain and frustration."*

"I concede. Next time I'll remember this diving lesson. Sometimes it's easier to build a bridge than to get a child into the bathtub," reflects Dad Shelby.

"What is similar is that if you make a mistake with a bridge or with a child, you can end up in hot water," quips Mom Shelby.

Second Chance: Turn to Scene 148

Goals

Rudolf Dreikurs, who provided the inspiration for most modern parenting programs, made children's misbehavior understandable. He discovered four goals of misbehavior. The first two goals are common and can be seen daily. The third and fourth goals present more serious challenges. For more information, each goal is discussed individually within this guide.

The Four Goals of Children's Misbehavior

Goal 1: Attention-getting
Goal 2: Power struggles
Goal 3: Revenge
Goal 4: Inadequacy

The Shelbys:

"I know this Rudolf Dreikurs. He claimed that by their sixth month most infants completely train their parents! They know exactly what to do to make adults respond predictably," says Mom Shelby.

"It's so much easier to see goals of misbehavior in action when Uncle William's kids are involved. They have Uncle Wallace and Aunt Williford eating out of their hands. You don't suppose our kids' misbehavior is goal-oriented too, do you?" asks Dad Shelby.

"I know they can make you dance like a puppet!" laughs Mom Shelby.

"Me! Not me! You make me so angry when you say things like that!" exclaims Dad Shelby.

"You see what I mean? You're easy to manipulate. I just succeeded."

"You set me up. That's not fair."

"That's exactly the point. Children know what to do to elicit certain reactions from us. Just like I know how to manage you. By the way, you should see what I bought at the Lingerie Lioness store for tonight," Mom Shelby purrs flirtatiously.

"I can't wait!" Dad Shelby rejoins. "Darn! There you go again! I can't believe how easy I am."

"Yes, in every way," Mom Shelby responds with a wink.

H

Homework

The most important factor in school success is modeling. When a family **value** supports a child's desire to learn, homework becomes a part of life. Both parents need not only to value, but also to model the importance of reading, learning, and discussing ideas. Below are four homework tips that will lead to success.

Homework Tips for Serious Families

- Create a quiet time when all media shuts down. During this period, *each* family member "studies." Parents can read, follow hobbies, or pursue other intellectual interests. If children have no homework, ask them to read, draw pictures,tell stories, or use creativity. Cultivate the inner life.

- Control television. Limit the amount of time a child watches television daily. Never allow a child to watch television during quiet time. Be vigilant. Television is addictive. An inner life cannot develop if television becomes a readily available substitute.

- Provide a desk or place for children to center their studies. They may study elsewhere, but they need a central location to help them organize their work.

- "Involvement, Not Interference" should be a parent's guide. Show your interest, but help children only when necessary. However, homework remains your children's job. Insist that they complete their work on their own unless they get stuck. Don't make them dependent on you by helping too much. The more you help, the less competent they may feel.

HOMEWORK CASE STUDY 1: The Brainless Addiction

"There you go again," mumbles Dad Shelby.

"What do you mean?" asks Mom Shelby.

"Suddenly you decide that the entire family needs to stop watching television so that William will do his homework. Bam! You turn off the set without a word of discussion!" Dad Shelby fires back.

*"Television is interfering with the children's school work. We need a family **value** that shows children daily that homework is more crucial than watching television."*

"You can't create a family value by yourself," rebuts Dad Shelby.

"Exactly. That's why I need your help. We need a quiet time on school nights when the television is off — even when the children claim they have no homework."

"I understand your point. But we need to work together on this. You sprang this idea on me in the middle of the most important game of the year. I hope you're not suggesting that we can never make exceptions to your quiet-time rule."

"No. Exceptions are fine. But we need to plan them in advance. Watching television needs to be contingent on finishing homework and chores. We need to plan ahead in our family meetings," explains Mom Shelby.

"I'm willing to talk. But don't expect me to give up major sporting events."

"We both value sports, and we both value education. We need to make agreements that show our children that BOTH are crucial. I'm afraid the children will watch anything on television at any time," adds Mom Shelby.

"Let's talk as soon as the game is over. Or, better still, I'll tape the last quarter and watch it later."

"Watch your game. I did spring this on you because I was totally frustrated. As long as I know that we will talk later about controlling television, I can wait."

"Tomorrow! New rules. I promise. Now let me return to those exciting Demon Deacons!" exclaims Dad Shelby.

Second Chance: Turn to Scene 144

HOMEWORK CASE STUDY 2: You Can Do Better Than That, Mom

"Don't even bother to tell me that I took over William's homework. Not only did I take over his project, but he then became my supervisor. Can you believe he was criticizing my ideas for HIS project? He never bothered to make a single suggestion," Mom Shelby complains.

"You tried to save a patient who wasn't really sick," observes Dad Shelby.

"I guess I felt flattered that he asked me for ideas. I love projects like this. Maybe it wouldn't have become a problem if he had liked my ideas."

"You would have had a worse problem then," Dad Shelby interjects.

"What do you mean?"

"Then you would have become Mrs. Creativity. In the future when William needs ideas, he will expect you to think for him. Helping is one thing, but taking over is another."

"Not to mention how unappreciated I feel. The more I do for my children, the more they expect me to do and the less appreciative they become."

"Maybe they're not appreciative because they really don't need your help. Make sure the patient is sick before you offer a cure," suggests Dad Shelby.

"I suppose I need to admit that your idea is good medicine. Next time I'll be sure William has done all he can do on his own before I rush to the rescue."

Second Chance: Turn to Scene 138

I

Inadequacy

Total discouragement! When children lose all hope, they give up. Sometimes their hopelessness is confined to a single academic subject, specific skill, or interpersonal experience. When totally discouraged, children resist offers of help and demand to be left alone.

Parents can recognize a child's declaration of inadequacy because adults, too will feel hopeless: "I've tried everything I can to help. Nothing works. I give up." Professional help is usually required when children surrender. The origin of the problem can be genetic, experiential, or a combination of the two. Professionals are trained to help children find the courage to succeed in the areas of their felt inadequacy.

The Shelbys:

"I don't understand inadequacy. How could any child feel totally incompetent? How could they give up?" Mom Shelby questions.

"Sweetheart, could you replace the fan belt in the car this afternoon?" Dad Shelby asks.

"Of course not. I don't know anything about cars. You know better than that. Cars are in your department. I've never understood anything about engines and I never will," replies Mom Shelby.

"It's easy. If you tried harder you could learn. I'll show you right this minute," Dad Shelby offers.

"NO! NO! NO! Leave me alone. I hate cars, and I don't want to understand them. Quit hounding me about those stupid engines. Who needs to know about fixing cars anyway? I'm never going to be a mechanic," wails Mom Shelby.

"True, but I see that you do understand feelings of inadequacy. Don't you?"

"Drat it! I hate it when you trick me!" exclaims Mom Shelby. *"But I get your point."*

Intelligence

In many ways, children are intellectually very different from one another. All have unique gifts. Some excel in one or more of the traditional academic areas such as math, science, language, or logic. Others' talents lead them to music or the performing arts. Still others may be gifted in creating interpersonal relationships and in helping people solve personal problems. Physical dexterity leads many toward activities such as athletics or gymnastics. **Encourage** all of your children and each of their interests. Celebrate the different gifts children exhibit.

Children are also alike in many ways. Cognitive psychologists believe children travel through different worlds of thought. Babies learn through touching and putting objects in their mouths. Preschoolers enjoy exciting imaginations but lack advanced logical abilities. In the middle years of elementary school, most children abandon the world of imagination and become more logical and extremely literal. During their teenage years, the majority of young people begin to think more symbolically and with increased complexity. Be patient. Enjoy each childhood world of thought.

The Shelbys:

"Different is right! William and Wally live in two opposite worlds. All Wally wants to do is play. He is so creative and inventive," observes Mom Shelby.

"Yeah, and all William wants to do is tell me when I make a mistake," Dad Shelby adds.

"William's not that bad. He's recently discovered that adults make mistakes and is excited to uncover them. You just blunder more bluntly than most people. Don't forget William used to play just like Wally does. Remember how he used to create those giant, pretend battles with all of his figures when he was four years old?" Mom Shelby reminds her husband.

"That's true. At least now he's interested in sports and fishing. He loves to learn exactly how to do things. I guess Ken West is right," observes Dad Shelby.

"What do you mean?"

"Each world of thought has its weaknesses."

"I'd rather think that each stage has its strengths!" Mom Shelby counters.

"Wow. Even we think totally differently," Dad Shelby acknowledges, as Mom Shelby nods in vigorous agreement.

J

Joking

Children's humor changes with age. In infancy, they enjoy physical games initiated by parents, such as being tickled. By age two, they can initiate humorous interactions themselves, such as playing chase. Three-year-olds love for parents to make wrong guesses and say silly things. Also, bathroom humor becomes important because toilet training has been a central part of the child's life. For instance, one youngster may call another child "Doo-doo head," and everyone laughs. (Those who work with college-age students will notice that some humor never changes!)

When children reach middle elementary school, they enjoy slapstick humor. Particularly they relish seeing adults falter. Popular children's books usually describe adult characters who continuously blunder, while the heroes are children blessed with infallible intelligence. Laughing at others' failures is not meant to be cruel. Young people are adjusting to the fresh realization that adults are not perfect and no one can follow rules flawlessly.

When children become teenagers, their humor becomes more sophisticated. They love puns and plays on words. And yes, their humor can frequently take on a cruel flavor!

The Shelbys:

"I feel better," acknowledges Mom Shelby.

"Why?" asks her husband.

"Last week one of our teachers was carrying an armful of books when she slipped on the top of a flight of steps. The books flew out of her hands, and she bounced to the bottom of the stairs. When she came to a stop, her students were laughing. I thought that these kids were absolutely vicious," admits Mom Shelby.

"They were certainly being insensitive."

"Yes. But they didn't think about her being hurt. They just thought it was funny to see an adult goof. After they discovered that she was injured, they were very concerned."

"I bet it hurt her feelings to hear them laugh. I know I go nuts when William laughs at my mistakes," confesses Dad Shelby.

*"You need to **communicate** that to William. Children need to know we have feelings too. Nevertheless, I realize now that children do not intentionally try to hurt people with their laughter. They're just reacting to strange situations,"* advises Mom Shelby.

"You're right. I guess that's why my golfing buddies and I laughed at Uncle William when he slipped hitting his tee shot and fell right on his behind," Dad Shelby snickers.

"Yep. Some humor never changes," sighs Mom Shelby.

K

Kicking, Hitting, and Biting

These are all natural responses of a frustrated child. Although natural, they are unacceptable. Parents need to help children learn better **communication skills** to share their frustration and aggressive feelings.

Taking **quality time out** to regain control provides a positive **logical consequence** when children cannot act appropriately in the presence of others. Do not make the length of time out unreasonable. Children learn better behavior only after they return to a social scene and are given encouragement for selecting more appropriate interactions. When children act aggressively, always check the model that adults provide. Children who see their parents act aggressively will be more aggressive in their own interactions.

The Shelbys:

"Do you remember how you laughed at me when I got frustrated with Wendy's temper tantrums? I yelled as loud as I could, 'We do not yell in this house!' I hate to admit it, but I wasn't the best model, was I?" asks Mom Shelby.

"Finally, you've admitted it. I have never understood why you didn't see that you were doing the same thing Wendy did — yelling when you became frustrated," Dad Shelby responds.

"I guess you are more logical, aren't you? You would probably notice if your interventions became illogical?" Mom Shelby taunts.

"Oh no. I can tell I am about to take a fall. Okay. What did I do?"

"Do you remember this morning when William hit Wally and you spanked William? What did you say to him?" questions Mom Shelby.

"I've forgotten, but I think I am about to be reminded."

"You said, 'William, the Shelbys do not hit people!' Then whack, you smacked him right on the bottom."

"Time out! That's true, but William stopped hitting Wally," Dad Shelby retorts.

"Time out is right! If you had used time out, then you would not have modeled that it's okay for bigger people who are frustrated to hit smaller people."

"That's it! I'm going to my workroom until supper," mumbles Dad Shelby.

"Why?"

"So I don't make any more mistakes now that I'm totally frustrated," Dad Shelby grumbles.

"The medicine doesn't taste good, but we're learning."

L

Logical Consequences

Along with natural consequences, logical consequences serve as an alternative to permissiveness and physical punishment. Logical consequences teach children to accept responsibility for their mistakes and misbehaviors.

The secret of a good consequence is its logical connection to the misbehavior. If a child breaks a window, it is not logical for him or her to lose television rights, endure a speech, or receive a spanking. None of these responses is related to the "crime." Paying for a new window, however, is both logical and educational.

After a two-year-old child rushes into the street, logic dictates that the child loses the right to play outside for a period of time. Then, when the child is allowed outside play again, parents need to quickly **encourage** him or her for playing within the rules. Other alternatives can be less educational and lead to more difficulties. For example, swatting a child leads to **power struggles** and lectures lead to **permissiveness.**

When raised to accept the natural and logical consequences of behaviors, in time young people begin to ask: What will be the consequences of my making this decision? Am I willing to accept these consequences? Or, having made a mistake, they will ask: What is my logical responsibility to others for having made this mistake?

Consequences work best when they are made and agreed upon in advance. **Family meetings** provide a good opportunity, for example, to agree upon the future consequences of failing to do **chores**, **swearing**, missing curfews, **fighting**, or breaking important family rules.

When consequences cannot be agreed upon in advance, then parents must create a one-time consequence that connects the misbehavior with a logical consequence. In a power struggle, these one-time consequences will seem more like punishment to a child; but as long as parents are confident of the logical connection between the misbehavior and the consequence, they will feel confident in their discipline techniques.

I was raised in a family that used a combination of logic, physical punishment, and permissiveness. My wife and I took **parenting classes** before our three children were born. We began to think of ourselves, in part, as teachers who try to help children make responsible decisions. As a result, we began to use only logical and natural consequences. Although it is often difficult to think of "perfect" consequences, we did our best. Using consequences and **family meetings** made a dramatic difference in the atmosphere of our home. Nothing will bring you more satisfaction than to see your children eventually begin to be logical and fair in their own interactions with others.

Remember, consequences need to be logically connected to the misbehavior or mistake. Do not warn, threaten or moralize. Children need to trust you. When they misbehave, young people must know that consequences will follow as predictably and naturally as the sun sets in the evening.

LOGICAL CONSEQUENCES CASE STUDY 1: The Hand That Threw the Rock

"What did you learn from Wally's misbehavior?" Mom Shelby asks.

"You mean, what did Wally learn? He was the one who threw the rock through Mr. Carlson's window," Dad Shelby replies.

"Yes. But you were the one who took the consequences. Mr. Carlson enjoyed making you search for every sliver of glass."

"Mr. Carlson is such a jerk. I cannot believe he treated me so badly when I didn't even break his window," Dad Shelby complains.

"Maybe Mr. Carlson was just as confused as I was," suggests Mom Shelby.

"What do you mean?"

"I couldn't figure out why Wally was inside watching television while you were outside cleaning up the mess he made. Mr. Carlson was probably miffed that the perpetrator of the crime got off without accepting any apparent consequences," Mom Shelby explains.

"I guess I didn't want Mr. Carlson to have a chance to abuse Wally. I did intend to have Wally pay for the window, though," Dad Shelby says.

"I understand that you tried to protect Wally. However, I think you taught him the wrong lesson. What do you think Wally learned from this entire mess?" Mom Shelby asks.

"Okay! I see your point. I suppose Wally learned that when the going gets tough his parents will protect him and, worse, shield him from the public consequences of his misbehavior. Not only did I suffer by accepting Wally's consequences, but also I gave Wally a bad message," answers Dad Shelby.

"Maybe all is not lost. I bet the reader understands that we can offer support and even supervise their consequences, but in the end children need to be responsible for their own behaviors."

Second Chance: Turn to Scene 83

LOGICAL CONSEQUENCES CASE STUDY 2: Return to Mars

"I am so frustrated. William just doesn't seem to be able to plan anything in advance. No sooner do I return from rushing to the store to buy his poster paper than he informs me that he needs a red marker. I guess I'll try to find a store that's still open at this late hour. What has happened to William's memory?" asks Mom Shelby.

"You stole his memory," observes Dad Shelby.

"What on earth is your point?" snaps Mom Shelby.

"Why should William remember anything when he has a servant ready to do his bidding at any time? What a terrific bargain. William forgets. You take the consequences."

"This is school work, dear. William's project is due tomorrow. I'd be less than responsible not to help," Mom Shelby explains.

LOGICAL CONSEQUENCES

"You're doing more than helping. You're teaching William to wait until the last minute because he knows whatever he needs, you will provide despite what your plans may be. William isn't showing **respect for himself or others.**"

"What do you suggest I do — let William fail?" Mom Shelby asks sarcastically.

"You're making the situation sound like a potential catastrophe. You know that William would not fail. If you refused to go to the store, he would find another way to finish his project. Also, he would learn that if he waits until the last second, he'll need to depend on himself rather than you. I suggest that you resign as William's servant," Dad Shelby answers.

"Maybe you're right. But I don't feel like a good mother when I don't do all I can to help," counters Mom Shelby.

"Sometimes less is more. The less you help children who aren't being responsible, the more you teach them to be independent."

"I suppose I've had enough of William's procrastination. Okay, I resign as William's personal servant. Now, let me see if I can live with the guilt," Mom Shelby says.

"Wow! Does William ever have you trained! He doesn't prepare and you feel guilty," quips Dad Shelby.

"Okay. I get the point. As the saying goes, from now on a failure to plan ahead on William's part will not constitute a crisis on mine!"

Second Chance: Turn to Scene 146

LOGICAL CONSEQUENCES CASE STUDY 3: Empty Threats

"I felt like a worm on a fishing hook. No matter how I squirmed, things went from bad to worse. I thought Wally would take a bath if I threatened to make him sleep on plastic sheets. How could I have guessed that he might think plastic sheets would be fun?" mutters Dad Shelby.

"Things grew worse from there?" asks Mom Shelby.

"Absolutely. Then I tried to force him into the water. Wally changed from a **power struggle** to **revenge** faster than a piranha devours — well, a worm. But I should never have slapped Wally when he called me a liar. **Logical consequences** would have worked better," Dad Shelby answers.

"I agree. What consequences did you take for your misbehavior?"

"I didn't misbehave. I was just trying to give Wally a bath."

"Seems to me you made a promise to Wally that you didn't keep. As adults we call that an idle threat, but Wally gave it a playground name you didn't like," observes Mom Shelby.

"Wait a minute. I cannot believe you're saying I caused this problem," puffs Dad Shelby.

"No. It takes two to fight. You jumped into the ring, but you ended up fighting a world class combatant. You know better than to threaten children with consequences you don't intend to use."

"Why? What harm can come of it?" Dad Shelby innocently asks.

"I can't believe you are asking! Don't play naïve with me. Wally called your bluff and you paid a heavy price. How will he know in the future when you're serious or when you're just making threats?"

"But my plastic sheet consequence wasn't going to work," pleads Dad Shelby.

"Who knows? I think the novelty of plastic sheets would eventually wear off. But that's not the point. You're only as good as your word," Mom Shelby explains.

"I guess you're right. But Wally should never call me a liar," Dad Shelby says in an obvious attempt to save face.

"You're absolutely right. I'm sure you'll **communicate** that to him later. Wouldn't you love to have the opportunity to go back in time and play this scene over again?"

"No! I'd rather not be in that situation at all. But I suppose the reader will take me back anyway," Dad Shelby replies.

Second Chance: Turn to Scene 157

Lying

Children lie for many reasons. Preschoolers' imaginations may run wild. In these cases, the difference between lying and exaggeration becomes as clouded as it does in an adult's fish tales. At times, youngsters lie to avoid a punishment that frightens them. In some situations, children lie to make themselves appear to be more important or "bigger" in the eyes of others. At other times, children lie to defy those in authority.

Don't overreact. Lying is not a single test of moral virtue. Instead, it's a commentary on a child's thinking in a given situation. Confronting a lie usually proves to be fruitless. In fact, the more frequently a cornered child repeats a lie, the more likely he or she is to believe that the lie is the truth.

Humor works well: "I bet that line works on everyone!" Or, at times, acknowledge the lie but sidestep it: "I know you don't think I really believe that." In a crisis, children do not listen to moral lectures any more willingly than adults do.

Children's moral thinking grows more complex with age (see **cheating**). Parents need to model their family **values.** When children observe their parents being truthful in difficult situations, the example stays with them forever. "Little white lies" parents may tell ("Tell the phone caller that I'm not home.") show children that it's okay to lie in stressful situations. Be patient. Don't overreact. Provide a consistent, positive model.

LYING CASE STUDY: Bury More than the Cat

"Why do children have to be so observant? I felt so good about how I handled the Carlsons' cat situation," says Mom Shelby.

"You mean the dead cat situation. Don't forget our children murdered the Carlsons' cat," Dad Shelby replies.

"Don't make this worse. I know they killed the cat. I just didn't realize that by not facing up to the Carlsons I was just as guilty as the kids," explains Mom Shelby.

"I understand. You didn't want the Carlsons to be even more angry with you and our family."

"Exactly. I was afraid to tell the truth. But I didn't realize that until I thought about it later."

"You mean until Wendy saw right through you," Dad Shelby says.

"Don't rub it in. I guess even adults may not tell the truth when the consequences seem too chilling," Mom Shelby admits.

"That's true. What do you plan to do now?"

"At the least, I will explain my mistake to the children. I need to model telling the truth even in the most difficult situations. If I don't, I'm afraid they won't be honest with me when things become tough for them. I suppose we will also need to talk with the Carlsons."

"I don't think we've ever had a tougher situation. Not telling the truth to the Carlsons certainly would be easier in many ways — for all of us. But it's your call," Dad Shelby says.

"No. Now, it's the reader's call," counters Mom Shelby.

"To think that we told the children that telling the truth is always easier in the long run," Dad Shelby sighs.

Second Chance: Turn to Scene 93

M

Marriage

Arguably, the most important relationship in a family is the parents' marriage. As the marriage goes, so go the children. Time invested in strengthening a marriage becomes a gift to the entire family. Not only does a strong marriage model good **communications**, but it also allows children to feel security in a sometimes chaotic world. Children are just passing through their parents' home; spouses may remain together for decades to come.

When marital partners are not united psychologically, they encounter difficulty parenting together. As a result, one parent may become overly involved with the children and another underinvolved. Or, one adult may become extremely permissive and the other uncompromisingly authoritarian. At worst, children become trapped in the middle.

Disagreements between parents about their marital relationship need to be handled privately. When tension and animosity between parents boil over, their children begin to feel the tension. At times, a child may be drawn into the parents' fracas by either attempting to solve the adults' problems or by dysfunctioning in a way that draws the parents' antagonism away from one another.

Family therapy can help everyone escape from the tangled webs of marital and/or other relationship difficulties. Nothing, however, beats prevention. Take time for your marriage. A couple's investment in each other will yield high dividends for the children.

MARRIAGE CASE STUDY 1: Parental Split

"How dare you take out your frustrations on my daughter," says Mom Shelby.

"Your daughter. She's my daughter, too," shouts Dad Shelby.

As Dad Shelby's voice soars, the veins in his neck and face swell and a monstrous look overtakes him. "You're acting as if I'm out of control!" shrieks Dad Shelby.

Silence engulfs the couple. By chance Dad Shelby sees his own reflection in the bedroom mirror. A smile emerges. Then Dad Shelby breaks out in laughter. Mom Shelby joins him.

"I suppose I am out of control," admits Dad Shelby.

"At least we haven't lost our sense of humor. But we need to talk. The tension between us frightens the children," observes Mom Shelby.

"We rarely have time to talk. And we never go out by ourselves any more," Dad Shelby retorts with a slightly accusatory tone.

"I know. We've been so busy since I returned to work. I guess I've tried to spend all of my free time with the children."

"The less time you and I spend together, the more unhappy I feel. I'm afraid my discontent boils over at anyone who crosses me."

"You're right. We've been putting the children ahead of our marriage. Let's put ourselves first at least one night each week. I'll call a babysitter for tomorrow night," Mom Shelby offers.

"Finding a babysitter for the Shelby children will be as easy as finding volunteers for a tax audit. But we need our time alone. I feel better already just knowing we will have it. I'm sorry I blew up at Wendy."

"You can talk with her later. I'm sorry it took a bad incident to remind us where our priorities should be. The children shouldn't suffer because of our problems. I guess if we take care of our relationship, our children will benefit as well," concludes Mom Shelby.

"Maybe the reader can return to see that justice to Wendy is done," Dad Shelby hopes.

Second Chance: Turn to Scene 53

MARRIAGE CASE STUDY 2: William Enters the Lions' Den

"We cannot go on this way. You are too hard on the children, and I won't stand for it," Mom Shelby challenges.

"I'm too hard because you're too soft. William stuck his head into a place where it didn't belong. He needed discipline, and I know you wouldn't have lifted a finger, much less a hand," Dad Shelby volleys.

"Maybe William tried to save us from ourselves. We were fighting like children, and he had the courage to intervene," counters Mom Shelby.

"There you go again. You're always taking the children's side."

"I really don't mean to be taking their side over yours. I think the problem is with us and not with the children," explains Mom Shelby.

"Are you blaming our marriage?" asks Dad Shelby.

"No. I think we never have agreed on discipline techniques to use with the children. I think you're too severe, and you believe I'm too permissive. Frankly, we're probably both right. The problem is that the children are caught in between us," says Mom Shelby.

"Maybe we are stuck. Is there anything we can do about it?"

"Ken West believes **parenting classes** help parents compromise. I guess we could learn in a course or through **family therapy**," Mom Shelby answers.

"I'm willing to take classes. Besides, it would give us some time together away from home."

"But the best part is that our children won't be caught in the middle of our fights. William showed a lot of courage trying to stop our nastiness. He just didn't know how to handle two childish parents."

"Now that I think about it, William was brave. I'll talk to him about our plans and apologize. I wish this fight had never happened," says Dad Shelby.

"I just wish we had done something about our differences sooner. Poor William. Children suffer when their parents fight," Mom Shelby admits.

Second Chance: Turn to Scene 62

MARRIAGE CASE STUDY 3: Sacrificial Flame

"William's right. It's not his problem; it's our problem. William would never set a fire in this house unless something was severely troubling him. That something is us. I'm scared," says Mom Shelby.

"Kids do crazy things all the time. Why are you dragging us into this? William knows better than to set fires," Dad Shelby replies.

"Exactly. William does know better. That's the point. Starting a fire is no minor incident, and it's far from the first major problem we've had with the children. It's time for you and me to quit blaming William. We all need to go to counseling and get to the bottom of these problems," Mom Shelby concludes.

"I don't see why I need to go. William is the one who keeps getting into trouble."

"You are my husband, and you're part of this family. If you love me, you will go with me to **family therapy***. I'm not asking you; I'm telling you to do this for me — for us. I'm scared for my children. I'm frightened for us," pleads Mom Shelby.*

"I don't see how this discussion is helping readers go back and make a different choice."

"I don't care about helping the readers at this moment. This is about us. We need some coaching, and we need it now. Are you part of this marriage and family or not?" asks Mom Shelby.

"Okay. I'll go. But I don't need it. This is not the way this book was supposed to go. We're supposed to be here for our readers," Dad Shelby complains.

"We're supposed to be here for each other and for our children first. Our readers will work things out. It means a lot to me that you're willing to go with the family to counseling. Maybe our children will feel less turmoil," hopes Mom Shelby.

Second Chance: Turn to Scene 64

N

Natural Consequences

Along with logical consequences, natural consequences serve as an alternative to permissiveness and physical punishment. Natural consequences are the best learning experiences for people of any age.

A natural consequence occurs when parents do not intervene in a situation but allow the situation to teach the child. The technique is based on the adage: "Every generation must learn that the stove is hot."

NATURAL CONSEQUENCES

If ice cream is left on a counter, it melts. When children refuse to eat, they become hungry. If people stay awake too late at night, they will be tired the next day. When a child loses a baseball glove, she will not have a mitt for the next game. If, despite warnings from the lifeguard, a child runs beside the pool, he may fall and skin his knees. When children forget to take their lunch money to school, they will have nothing to eat.

In each of the cases above, the child learns from the natural consequences of his behavior. The experience becomes the teacher. Parents do not need to intervene. On the contrary, adults should refrain from saying anything, particularly variations on the "I told you so" theme. If parents intervene by lecturing or by dispensing additional punishment, they risk destroying the natural learning situation by creating **power struggles.**

Natural consequences always work, but at times, they can be too severe or the natural consequence can be too delayed to be effective. In these cases, **logical consequences** should be used. For example, the natural consequence of running into the street is obviously unacceptable. Not allowing the child to play outside for a period of time offers a more logical consequence. Failure to brush one's teeth will result in cavities. However, that natural consequence will occur too late to be a deterrent. Therefore, not allowing sweets to children who refuse to brush their teeth works more effectively.

The most effective discipline parents can provide allows nature to run its course. Bite your tongue. Don't offer additional punishment. Simply allow the natural consequences of a child's behavior to be the teacher.

NATURAL CONSEQUENCES CASE STUDY 1: A Ticket for Your Troubles

"I'm a lightning rod for trouble," Mom Shelby proclaims.

"Actually, you just haven't learned that each generation must learn that the stove is hot," counters Dad Shelby.

"I resent your saying that. You know that I accept responsibility for my mistakes," snaps Mom Shelby.

"Yes, but you accept responsibility for everyone else's, too. When you're too helpful, you rob the new generation of the opportunity to realize that the stove is hot," Dad Shelby explains.

"Wendy needed my help. I just didn't have time to help her. That's why I was rushing and the policeman gave me a ticket."

"I see it differently," Dad Shelby begins.

"What do you mean?"

*"You were not showing **respect for yourself and others.** By allowing Wendy's mistakes to make you late for work, you showed a lack of respect for yourself. To believe Wendy couldn't handle her own problems showed a lack of respect for her."*

"Since I took my job, I feel as if I need to help the children when I can," explains Mom Shelby.

*"Yes. But in this case, you couldn't help without punishing yourself and your colleagues. Maybe we need to have more **family meetings** to help the children plan better and to talk about their accepting more responsibility," Dad Shelby suggests.*

"So you think I'm being overly responsible and actually making them less responsible. Maybe you're right. But it's tough to see my children unhappy," Mom Shelby says.

"True, but they need to learn early about responsibility. If they don't, we'll be cleaning up their messes for the rest of our lives. We both need to practice distinguishing when the problem is theirs and when it's yours or mine."

"You're right. Let's call a meeting and talk about responsibility. From now on, I'm going to let them solve their own problems. By the way, Wally called. He left his baseball bat at home. Should we run it over to the park?" Mom Shelby wonders aloud. Then she laughs: "There I go again!"

Second Chance: Turn to Scene 13

NATURAL CONSEQUENCES CASE STUDY 2: Eat Beans or Be Beaten

"How hungry would you have been?" asks Mom Shelby.

"What do you mean?" Dad Shelby replies.

"If Wally had not eaten, how hungry would you have become?"

"I see. You're saying that eating or not eating was Wally's problem and not mine," concludes Dad Shelby.

"Exactly. All we need to do is to clear Wally's plate after dinner, then refuse to allow snacks. What do you suppose would happen then?" Mom Shelby guides in a slightly condescending tone.

"Wally would be hungry and whine," Dad Shelby explains.

"Yes, and the whining simply shows the natural consequence is working. I bet he would eat a good breakfast the next morning. Then tomorrow night at supper, he would realize that the penalty for not eating is his own hunger."

*"You're right. I jumped into a **power struggle** instead of letting nature handle the problem. Sometimes it's hard for me to step back and not be controlling."*

"Ironically, you were being controlled. Wally knows exactly how to set your temper ablaze. Unfortunately, the power struggle kept his mind off of eating," Mom Shelby says.

"I'm not willing to ruin everyone's supper again! I like your plan. From now on, eating is Wally's problem, not mine," declares Dad Shelby.

"Good! I'll make sure Wally doesn't eat filling snacks before dinner. Then we'll let nature do its work."

"I agree. It's ironic that the best discipline we can provide sometimes is to do nothing at all. Tomorrow, I'll hold my tongue," Dad Shelby promises.

"Maybe the reader will give you another chance before then."

Second Chance: Turn to Scene 108

NATURAL CONSEQUENCES CASE STUDY 3: 7, 8, 9, 10! Now You've Had It!

"Congratulations! You may be the first parent who ever reached 10! On most nights Wally comes to dinner before you reach seven. You should have seen your face as you came closer and closer to the forbidden number," exclaims Dad Shelby.

"I don't need your sarcasm. I'm sick of this game. Every night I have to beg or threaten people to come to dinner. That's so disrespectful. I feel as if my work is totally unappreciated," Mom Shelby declares.

"Obviously, we need to do something different. Since this case study is in the natural consequence section, I suppose we should try a natural consequence," suggests Dad Shelby.

"I'm game. And I know what it's going to be. William can tell time. From now on, I'm going to announce when supper will begin, and we'll eat without him if he's not back on time."

"What if he forgets to wear his watch?"

"Tough. Being here is his responsibility, not mine. William has made his presence at supper my problem. No longer. Being at supper is William's problem. He'll have to keep in touch with the time. I refuse to be his clock," Mom Shelby replies.

"What if he doesn't eat with us?" asks Dad Shelby.

"He'll go hungry for the night. I'm not warming up supper for an ungrateful child. Sooner or later he'll get the message. No more games! No more catering to rascals!" Mom Shelby resolves.

"I'm glad Ken West put this in the natural consequence section. Going ahead with dinner is certainly reasonable. And your plan will work better than having William push you to the brink every evening," says Dad Shelby.

"We'll see. I can't wait to put my strategy into action."

Second Chance: Turn to Scene 99

NATURAL CONSEQUENCES CASE STUDY 4: One Entrée from Victory

Mom Shelby hangs her head and picks up the telephone in the kitchen: "Is this Ken West?"

"Mom Shelby! It's great to hear from you. How are those consequences working?" the author innocently asks.

"You know exactly how they're working; you're writing the book. Instead of begging William to come in from supper, I just went ahead with our meal. When William came in late he complained about the cold food, and I just couldn't keep my mouth shut."

"You sound as if you know exactly what turned a good natural consequence into a **power struggle.**"

"My mouth. I was so frustrated that I just had to have the last word," Mom Shelby says.

"And did you enjoy the last word? That would be a rare pleasure with a child," observes Ken West.

"Of course I didn't. William yelled the next last word and left the room. I know you'll ask me what would have happened if I had said nothing. The natural consequence would have probably worked."

"I think so too. You set up the consequence beautifully, and even cleared the house of snacks. Look at the positive: You did a terrific job and were almost there. You learned from this experience to resist the last word temptation. Last words offer a few seconds of enjoyment and a night full of disaster."

"What should I do now?" asks Mom Shelby.

"What do you think you should do?"

"I think I should ask for Dad Shelby's help. Then we should add a discussion about attending supper to the **family meeting.** I'll explain that supper will start at a certain time, and everyone needs to be responsible to be there. Having an agreement in advance will help me be quiet when anyone protests."

"I agree 100 percent. You're really catching on fast. In fact, I think that your consequence would have worked anyway, if you could have resisted the last word temptation. Maybe we'll have the opportunity to see."

Second Chance: Turn to Scene 126

NATURAL CONSEQUENCES CASE STUDY 5: Pride Precedes Surrender

"I know this problem all too well," Mom Shelby admits.

"What do you mean?" asks Dad Shelby.

"Your pride led you to fall victim to the last word temptation. Wally chose to wash his hair with regular shampoo. You warned him that it could sting his eyes. After it did, Wally tried to shift the blame," says Mom Shelby.

*"And I fell into the trap. I couldn't resist telling Wally that the outcome was his fault — the ol' last word temptation. As soon as I opened my mouth, I swallowed his bait and a **power struggle** raged. It's so hard to just be quiet and let a child's storm blow itself out."*

"Believe me, I know. But for a natural consequence to work, parents need to keep their tongues from wagging. When children are born, I think they activate a parental 'I told you so' gene!" Mom Shelby teases.

"Isn't that the truth! If I had to do it over again, I would bite my tongue and say nothing. Wally would have ranted and raved for a few minutes. But in the end nature would have taught him an important lesson."

Second Chance: Turn to Scene 154

O

Ordinal Position

Most parents sense that birth position is important to children. Oldest, middle, only, and youngest children each experience a different family environment and unique life circumstances. Unfortunately, mistaken mythology about ordinal position grows as quickly as kudzu in the southern countryside. There is no way to predict exactly what personality each child in a family will develop. However, the following guidelines may be of interest to you:

Guidelines Governing Ordinal Position

- Each child in a family seeks a place of uniqueness. Therefore, children in a family are usually extremely different in personality and interests.

- Where one child succeeds, others will not venture unless a family **value** exists in that area. If not discouraged, children will be most similar in the area of their family's values.

- If within four years of each other in age, first and second children are usually opposites in personality except where family values exist. Therefore, one cannot predict what the characteristics of the oldest two children will be, only that they will "divide the turf."

- One family can have several constellations. Whenever a four-year gap exists between two children, another constellation begins. (For instance, if children are 18, 16, 11, and 8, then there are two sets of first and second children.)

- If one child in a family excels in too many positive areas, then another child may become discouraged and find his or her place by being the "best at being worst."

- Only children grow up quickly in a world of adults. As long as they routinely practice cooperating and sharing with other children, they usually grow up to be self-confident, caring, and successful.

- Parents can help all of their children by creating family values, eliminating comparisons, using **encouragement** instead of criticism, accepting individual differences, and helping each child find a positive place of uniqueness.

The Shelbys:

"That explains it," says Mom Shelby.

"Explains what?" asks Dad Shelby.

"I have always thought it was amazing how different our children are. William and Wendy act as if they were raised on different planets."

"Maybe they were! They are opposites. But they don't seem to compete. They don't even like the same activities. William absolutely loves school, and Wendy couldn't care less. Of course, she has all the friends. What a social butterfly!"

"Maybe that's the point. They split the territory. Where one succeeded, the other did not try to excel. Maybe we should look at our family values more closely. I think academics and friendships are equally important," suggests Mom Shelby.

"O.K. I hear what you're saying about William's and Wendy's interests," begins Dad Shelby, carefully ignoring his wife's reference to family values. He continues, "But how do you explain Wally? He wants to be the best at everything!"

"He sure does. But he doesn't always want to work hard. What he seems to be best at is charming everyone else into doing things for him — especially his mother and father! He's becoming Mr. Personality," Mom Shelby explains.

"Yes, but when Wally does well at something, he'll work on it forever. I think Wally will be terrific when he decides exactly what he wants to accomplish. Besides, you and I recognize when he's trying to charm us into doing his work," Dad Shelby proclaims.

"Dad, can you help me put together this airplane. You're the best put-it-togetherer in the world," interrupts Wally.

"Sure, Wally. I'd love to do it for you," Dad Shelby proudly responds as he reaches for Wally's plane.

"You're right, dear. You are good at resisting Wally's charm," laughs Mom Shelby.

P

Parenting Classes

In nine years of higher education, no course added more to my life than the non-credit parenting course my wife and I took as graduate students. In parenting classes, we learned many of the basic concepts presented in this book. Isn't it ironic that many schools prepare students least for the most important challenges in their lives — marriage and raising children? Whether you have a house full of children or plan to begin a family later, take a parenting course if the opportunity arises. It may be the most important time you'll ever spend in class.

The Shelbys:

"That's the last thing I wanted to hear," declares Dad Shelby.

"What do you mean?" asks Mom Shelby.

"I did not want to hear how great parenting classes are. When the Carlsons posted notices about parenting classes on our front door, I swore I would never attend."

"That's exactly how I felt. But I'm impressed. Our friend Ken West has taken a ton of courses. For him to say that an inexpensive, non-credit course changed his life impresses me."

"Don't you think it would be embarrassing to talk about our children's behavior in front of other people?"

"My guess is that all of us face the same challenges with our children. In fact, I bet attending classes will show us how normal our children are," replies Mom Shelby.

"I hope not. If our children are normal, then in a few years this planet will need major rehabilitation," laughs Dad Shelby.

Permissiveness

Permissive parents are kind and caring. They are sensitive to the needs of their children and are in tune with their feelings. Relationships are important to permissive parents, and they care about their children's thoughts and feelings. Permissive parents possess important strengths. However! Weaknesses of permissive parents fall in the area of discipline. Rules and consequences for breaking them are rarely created and/or executed. Children who are not allowed to learn responsibility by facing the consequences of their mistakes and misbehavior, at worst, run wild and fail to respect the rights of others. When a child demands, "I want what I want when I want it," permissive parents eventually surrender. Although indulgent parents may believe that their children are misunderstood, everyone else understands that these children are tyrants.

Talking rather than taking action is the major characteristic of permissive discipline. Parents plead, beg, reason, and bargain until they exhaust everyone's patience. Rather than facing the consequences of their behavior, tyrannical children are frequently rewarded with bribes and special privileges for doing chores and daily activities that should be expected responsibilities. Ironically, parents frequently accept the consequences of their children's misbehavior and feel overwhelmed and used.

Permissive parents possess crucial strengths in communications and sensitivity. However, permissiveness in discipline can be a difficult weakness to overcome. Some parents can learn on their own to use **natural** and **logical consequences**, **family meetings**, and good **communication** skills. Others benefit from **parenting classes** or family counseling.

Permissive parents love their children. They need to love them more. How? To flourish, children need to develop **respect for themselves and others**, as well as to accept the consequences of their behavior. Parents, not teachers, neighbors, friends, or the authorities, should be children's most important teachers.

PERMISSIVENESS CASE STUDY 1: Who is the Real Monster?

"I feel like such a monster. I know that field trip was important to Wendy, but I didn't have time to go back home to retrieve her form. I just cannot be late for work again. Can you believe Wendy kicked me in front of a teacher?" sobs Mom Shelby.

"There was a monster at work this morning, but it wasn't you," observes Dad Shelby.

"You cannot mean little Wendy."

"Yes, I do. She may be small, but she thinks she's a giant. I hate to say it, but I think on this morning a monster was temporarily created. Wendy wanted what she wanted when she wanted it. She didn't care about anyone else's needs or rights."

*"I did give in to her. But I was just trying to buy some peace. That's why I **bribed** her with pancakes to push her to dress faster," explains Mom Shelby.*

"Didn't you offer her a ride to school when she chose to move too slowly to catch the bus?" asks Dad Shelby.

"If you're asking if I gave in to her during every crisis, I did. But I did confront her when she demanded that I return home to get the permission slip for the field trip. How could she be so angry at me when I tried so hard to help?"

PERMISSIVENESS

*"I think by giving in to Wendy's unreasonable demands and behavior, she began to expect you to serve her. She doesn't believe she should accept the **logical consequences** for any of her misbehaviors. She expects us to bail her out of trouble every time she makes mistakes," concludes Dad Shelby.*

"But that's so illogical," Mom Shelby replies.

"Maybe not. We're the ones who keep pampering her. She believes if we don't do what she demands, then we're awful and unfair."

"I did create a monster. By trying to save the peace, I brought on a humiliating war. After I stood up to her, I should have driven off and let her handle the problem. She would have been mad, but at least I would not have been publicly abused."

"And Wendy would have learned that she must assume responsibility for her own mistakes," notes Dad Shelby.

*"You're right. Monsters want what they want when they want it. No more. From now on, I'll show **respect for myself and others**," Mom Shelby proclaims.*

"Yes, we need to show Wendy that she is old enough to accept the consequences of her actions."

"And her lack of action," adds Mom Shelby.

Second Chance: Turn to Scene 13

PERMISSIVENESS CASE STUDY 2: Barking up the Wrong Tree

"What in the world was behind that phone call?" Mom Shelby asks.

"William went over the fence into the Carlsons' yard and teased their dog again. Apparently, Liberty forgot he was chained and raced until the chain yanked him backwards and almost snapped off his head. Then Liberty knocked over the Carlsons' ceramic deer herd," laughs Mr. Shelby.

"That's terrible. And, it's not funny. Poor Liberty. That was really mean of William. No one should treat animals that way."

"What about how people should treat kids? Mr. Carlson called our kids 'lousy,'" Dad Shelby says defensively.

"William was lousy to Liberty. I heard your conversation with Mr. Carlson, and I think you were lousy, too," flares Mom Shelby.

"What should I have done?" snaps Dad Shelby.

"What I hope you will do right this minute. Call Mr. Carlson and acknowledge that William was wrong. Let Mr. Carlson know that you will discipline William."

"Do I have to?"

"Mr. Carlson was right. You are being childish," Mom Shelby observes.

"Brother. I guess Mr. Carlson got the best of me again," sighs Dad Shelby.

"No. William hurt his dog. This situation is not about your and Mr. Carlson's egos."

"Okay. Give me the phone," Dad Shelby concedes. "Sometimes I hate it when you're right."

Second Chance: Turn to Scene 55

PERMISSIVENESS CASE STUDY 3: The Banana Splits the Children

"I wonder what got into Wendy. All I did was offer Wally a banana split for finishing his supper," says Dad Shelby.

"I'll tell you exactly what got into me!" announces Wendy Shelby.

"Wendy Shelby, you're not supposed to appear in this part of the book. I want you to leave this instant!" demands Dad Shelby.

"I bet if I were Wally you wouldn't make me leave," replies Wendy.

"What is that supposed to mean?" asks Dad Shelby.

"You play favorites. You allow Wally to get away with murder. If William and I did the things Wally does, then we'd stay in our rooms forever. I cannot believe you offered Wally a banana split just to eat. You told William and me it was up to us whether or not we eat. You said we would have to suffer some kind of dumb **natural consequence** for not eating, but it was our choice."

"Maybe you're right. I shouldn't **bribe** Wally. But my mistake didn't give you the right to sling beans at Wally. Why did you make such a mess?" Dad Shelby attacks.

"Because William and I hate Wally when you play favorites. He's a spoiled brat, and we can't stand him," yells Wendy.

"Don't you call your brother a spoiled brat!" Dad Shelby shouts.

"Sweetheart," begins Mom Shelby. "I think you need to listen to Wendy's message. She feels as if you're playing favorites by being more permissive with Wally. Favoritism creates friction and bad feelings."

"Wendy, that's not true. I love each of you the same," says Dad Shelby.

"Then please treat us the same. Are you going to take Wally out for a banana split or not?" Wendy hammers.

"Gee, I wish I had never offered. You're right. I made a mistake. No banana splits for anyone. And, in the future eating meals is each person's responsibility. Okay?"

Wally, who has overheard the conversation, begins to shriek. "I suppose the little king hates to be dethroned," Wendy says venomously.

"How can I get myself out of this?" Dad Shelby mumbles.

Second Chance: Turn to Scene 108

Physical Punishment

Parents who use physical punishment are not afraid to stand up to their children. They know when "enough is enough." Being able to take action when misbehavior occurs is an important strength.

The downside of using physical punishment is that it may lead to **power struggles** and **revenge**. Also, psychologists have discovered negative side effects when physical punishment is used frequently. Many children resort to **lying** when they believe punishment is illogical or too severe. In addition, because of their parents' modeling, physically punished children who are stronger and in control tend to hit and bully younger children.

Adults who use physical punishment tend to learn quickly how to substitute **logical** and **natural consequences.** Consequences provide an active way to handle misbehavior and avoid permissiveness. Not only do consequences work, but also their use does not lead to undesirable side effects. Try consequences. I believe you will prefer them.

The Shelbys:

"I've learned my lesson," explains Mom Shelby, "but I just didn't know what else to do."

"Are you talking about your famous super-spankings (see Scene 19)?" asks Dad Shelby.

"Yes. You know I was raised with parents who really believed in physical punishment. I absolutely love my parents. But I never felt right hitting my own kids," confesses Mom Shelby.

"But it works! Well, sometimes it works," points out Dad Shelby.

"Actually, spanking always seems to cause more trouble than it's worth. I feel lousy. The kids are angry and won't talk to me afterwards. I'm willing to try something different."

"But you can't let kids get away with misbehavior. They need discipline."

*"You're exactly right. But spanking is only one discipline technique. **Natural and logical consequences** make a lot of sense to me. In fact, I believe it's tougher discipline in many ways. What I like about using consequences is that children learn something and don't end up as angry with me," says Mom Shelby.*

"Maybe it's right for you. But if spanking was good enough for Granddad Shelby, it's good enough for me!" Dad Shelby vows.

"Granddad Shelby also ate a heavy diet of red meat and smoked cigarettes until he couldn't breathe."

"Yes. But in those days people didn't know about the dangers of smoking and eating high fat diets. These are different times. Education changes things," Dad Shelby rebuts.

"That's exactly my point, dear. Let's try something new."

Power Struggles

NO! As soon as children learn this word, power struggles escalate and frustrated parents flood parent study programs. When strong-willed parents collide with strong-willed children, warfare frequently results.

Although parents generally dislike power struggles, children love them. Imagine the joy a forty-pound child takes in being able to turn a respectable adult into a fighting, screaming, uncontrolled giant. In a matter of seconds, most children can drag parents down to their level and defeat them.

Adults can never win a power struggle with a child. Why? Because children do not have to play by adult rules. Even when parents appear to have defeated a child, the child will frequently seek **revenge** and eventually punish the parent. After power struggles end, parents feel miserable and the family's harmonious atmosphere is ruined.

There are no winners in power struggles. Unfortunately, many parents take years to find this out. Wanting to believe that victory is possible, they draw battle lines in the sand or cross over the child's well-drawn lines and hope to be victorious. Yet the conclusion is always the same: Adults never win.

How should parents handle power struggles? The first rule is to free yourself from the child's control. Refuse to be dragged into the emotional gutter where you have no chance of victory. As soon as you feel yourself growing angry, ask yourself, "How can we both end up winning?" When children resort to emotions, adults need to continue to think.

Look for alternatives to fighting. Here are a few that may be helpful. With younger children, play **games** instead of fighting. With all children, use **communication** skills to reflect feelings. Give up your need to "enjoy" the last word in an argument. When your temper flares, simply walk away from the struggle. If you are on the verge of losing control, retreat to the bathroom and lock the door. Wait until you are in control, then talk with the child when a crisis no longer rages.

Frequently, parents can sidestep power struggles and allow **natural** or **logical consequences** to teach a child. Also, the family can discuss problems during the **family meeting**. Good luck! Remember, when it comes to power struggles, adults never win.

POWER STRUGGLES

POWER STRUGGLES CASE STUDY 1: The Shelbys Don't Hit!

"Classic! Perfect!" Dad Shelby taunts.

"What could you possibly be talking about? This was an absolutely horrible morning. Wendy refused to get up. Then when I tried to dress her, she slapped me. And who ended up getting the worst of a bad situation? Me. I fell on the floor and have a strawberry the size of a baby elephant's head on my elbow. What's perfect about awfulness?" Mom Shelby roars.

"Your confrontation became a classic! Ken West is right. You can never win a power struggle with a child," Dad Shelby answers.

"I wasn't trying to win. I was trying to make Wendy dress."

"Exactly. What a battle of the wills! The more you pushed Wendy to dress, the more she refused to comply. My favorite part was when you said the Shelbys don't hit. Then you whacked her!"

"You're not being helpful. Okay. You're right. That was a power struggle, and I was thrashed. Do you have any positive ideas for me or not?" a volatile Mom Shelby challenges.

*"I know that I shouldn't gloat over your warfare. But I'm the one who usually leaps into the power struggle gutter. I suggest that we talk about the children's **waking and sleeping** routines. We need a better system," replies Dad Shelby.*

*"You're exactly right. Why don't you and I talk first, then hold a **family meeting** after we create a plan?"*

*"Okay. I'm sure that more **logical consequences** connected to not getting up and refusing to dress in the morning will work better than **physical punishment**," suggests Dad Shelby.*

"Maybe so. And now that I know things are going to be better in the mornings, I can see why you thought the confrontation was funny. I guess if I give Wendy a Mom Shelby superwhack, then I can't tell her that the Shelbys don't hit," laughs Mom Shelby.

"I'm sorry I laughed. Sometimes humor is all that gets us through. I know if you could go back you would handle this situation differently."

"You bet. I just hope to have the chance to try again," pleads Mom Shelby.

Second Chance: Turn to Scene 1

POWER STRUGGLES CASE STUDY 2: Bookshelf Waterloo

"Wow! I'm in awe. My power struggles are minor league compared to yours: a smashed airplane, a cracked bookshelf, two smacked kids, and a father with a major limp," observes Mom Shelby.

"Wally played me like the proverbial fiddle. After I whacked him and sent him to his room, he knocked that bookshelf over on purpose. Then he tortured me by picking the books up slowly — one by one. Sometimes I think Wally's smarter than I am," moans Dad Shelby.

Mom Shelby wisely ignores an obvious response. "When it comes to power struggles, Wally's a wizard. When did you know things were going from bad to worse?"

"Not 'til I was neck-deep in dynamite. When I grow angry, I stop thinking and just react. Whatever I do next, I usually regret," confesses Dad Shelby.

"Give yourself credit. You did think about time out, but it wasn't **quality time out**. You connected the time out with **physical punishment,** which escalated the power struggle."

"I know. I could hear my father's voice in mine when I lost control and yelled at Wally. I'm learning new ways to handle a problem, but I need time to think."

"We're getting better. Sometimes we make mistakes, but at least we can talk about them afterwards. Soon practice will make perfect," Mom Shelby says.

"Well, not perfect. But I know more options now. I just need to count to ten until I can think of the best way to handle a problem. You're right; new habits will form soon. Next time I will do better."

Second Chance: Turn to Scene 49

POWER STRUGGLES CASE STUDY 3: Tear-full Shampoo

"Playing games with Wally worked to a point. But when he insisted on washing his own hair, I ran out of patience," explains Dad Shelby.

"Yes. Unfortunately, you also fell into an ocean of trouble!" Mom Shelby replies.

"You're exactly right. I knew I was in trouble the second I escalated the power struggle. I raced down a pier instead of over a bridge."

"If you could go back in time, how would you handle things differently?" Mom Shelby asks.

"The problem started when I ran out of patience. I needed to realize that power struggles always are piers to nowhere. I knew Wally could wash his hair, and I should have encouraged him. **Encouragement** is a bridge that always ends on solid ground," Dad Shelby answers.

"I agree. That's easier to see with hindsight. It's tougher when we are frustrated."

"True, but there was a point when I knew I was headed for trouble and didn't have the courage to change directions. When I face that situation again, I need to look for the bridge," says Dad Shelby.

"Maybe our readers will help," Mom Shelby suggests.

Second Chance: Turn to Scene 152

Q

Quality Time Out

Quality time out was never intended to be punishment. Instead, quality time out offers children the opportunity to regain control of their emotions and behavior. Literally, it means to take time out.

Unfortunately, time out loses much of its quality and effectiveness when adults use the technique as punishment. As punishment, the technique's purpose is to make a child suffer rather than for him to take time to regain control of his emotions and behavior. When time out is used to punish children, **power struggles** and acts of **revenge** usually follow.

Tips for the Use of Quality Time Out

- Avoid using time out as punishment.

- Remove children from the situation that ignited their misbehavior. I prefer to use a child's bedroom or a room that is not aversive for time out. To use a chair or unnecessary confinement may create power struggles and frequently fails to remove a child from the source of his frustrations.

- On the first offense, do not use a timer. Allow the child to return as soon as he or she is in control. Remember, quality time out is not punishment. If a child returns to a situation immediately and behaves well, then the technique succeeds.

- When a child returns and behaves well, reinforce his positive behavior immediately. Children learn what not to do by going to time out. Upon returning to the action, they learn what they should do from our positive reinforcement.

- If a child returns and repeats the misbehavior, use a timer for the second offense. Be sure rules and consequences are understood in advance.

- Keep the time out period brief. Remember, the purpose of time out is for children to return to the situation in order to practice appropriate behavior.

- If a child misbehaves during time out, reset the timer. Five minutes of time out means five good minutes.

- Always let children know that they are responsible for their decisions: "I see you have decided that you need time out to regain control," or "I see you have decided you need the timer reset." Be brief. Avoid speeches that can lead to power struggles.

• If children "trash" their rooms or misbehave during time out, add **logical consequences**. "Your time is up. After you put things back where they belong, come join us."

The Shelbys:

"That's why my time outs don't work well!" exclaims Mom Shelby.

"What do you mean?" Dad Shelby asks.

"I've been using time out as a threat and for punishment. It seems so obvious from the name, but I never thought that the term literally meant to take time out to regain control. That makes a lot of sense."

"But what if a child comes out of his room immediately? What has he learned then?"

"The point is: What does he do when he leaves time out? If he behaves better, then time out served its purpose," explains Mom Shelby.

"But it seems as if he should have to stay longer."

"That's because you're still thinking in terms of punishment. We're not trying to hurt our children by using time out. We're letting them know that they cannot rejoin us until they change their behaviors," Mom Shelby continues.

"I suppose you don't think I should make them sit in a chair and face the wall either?" Dad Shelby pouts.

"Not unless you want to punish them. If you do, they'll punish you in return. Think how bad our atmosphere becomes after you yell at Wally a hundred times to get back in the chair and look at the wall. Quality time out teaches children they must behave to rejoin the family. That's the result we want!"

"What about time out for parents? It seems as if I should be able to take time out when I'm upset," Dad Shelby says.

"Yes. I think you should. It's far better than getting angry and saying something you will regret," Mom Shelby agrees.

"Good. I'll see you later. I'm going for a walk and think this through before I say something we'll both regret."

"Thanks!" replies Mom Shelby.

R

Respect for Self and Others (Mutual Respect)

To judge the appropriateness of any decision, ask two questions: Did I show respect for others? Did I respect myself?

Parents can show disrespect for children in many ways. They can be overly demanding. At times, requests may not be age-appropriate. For instance, to ask a preschool child to sit quietly through a long, "boring" speech or performance is disrespectful. To expect perfection of children also shows a basic disrespect for their well-being (see **Utopia**).

Disrespect can also be shown when parents expect too little from children. For example, parents should expect children to accept the consequences of their behavior and to perform age-appropriate **chores**.

Listen to your tone of voice. If you would not like to be talked to in the tone of voice you are using, you're probably not showing respect for your child.

Parents need to display respect for themselves, too. When parents sacrifice too much for others, family therapists call it "de-selfing." When parents de-self, they feel overwhelmed, used, and abused. Do not accept the consequences for your children's behaviors and mistakes. You have rights, too. Respect yourself and respect others.

RESPECT FOR SELF AND OTHERS CASE STUDY 1: Late for Wally's Sake

"I was fifteen minutes late to work. My principal was mad at me. I was mad at me. I cannot believe I promised Wally I would talk with his teacher before school. The teacher was busy ... well, I should have gone on to work and talked to her another time," Mom Shelby concludes.

"Why didn't you?" asks Dad Shelby.

"I promised Wally, and I couldn't let him down," Mom Shelby explains.

"Sounds as if you let yourself down. Out of respect for yourself, you should have gone to your job on time. That would have shown respect for yourself, your principal, your students, and Wally," Dad Shelby observes.

"Wally? What do you mean?"

"Wally needs to learn that he cannot have his way all the time. He must learn to handle life when it doesn't go as he plans," Dad Shelby answers.

"You're right. But I can't believe he insisted that I stay."

"People take advantage of their advantages. Don't blame Wally for asking you to stay. People will constantly ask you to do things for them that are not in your best interests. They have that right. You have the right to say no. Say no to them and yes to yourself," Dad Shelby explains.

"Exactly. Sometimes I act as if I have obligations and everyone else has rights. I can see your point about Wally, too. When I overly protect him, I make him dependent. That's disrespectful."

"We agree. Now, could you go to the store and buy some soft drinks? I'm going to work out and we've run out of drinks," Dad Shelby asks.

"NO! I'm too busy. Out of respect for myself, I'm going to say no to you," Mom Shelby responds gleefully.

"Drat! Why do you have to practice on me? Why couldn't you just return to the story like you're supposed to?"

Second Chance: Turn to Scene 38

RESPECT FOR SELF AND OTHERS CASE STUDY 2: My Way or No Way

"I'm sick of reading Green Eggs and Ham with Wally. I was just saying try another book, you'll like it, you'll see" explains Dad Shelby.

"But he didn't enjoy the new book. It was too complicated. Children Wally's age love repetition. You force-fed him a book inappropriate for his age," Mom Shelby responds.

"Give me a break. I told him we'd read his old book if he didn't like the new one."

"Yes, you did tell him that. When Wally grew bored, did you switch to his book?"

"No, I didn't. I wanted to read something new," responds Dad Shelby.

"Whose reading time was this?" asks Mom Shelby.

"It was ours. I guess I wasn't being respectful of Wally's needs. I focused too much on my own frustration," Dad Shelby answers.

"I agree. There was no harm done. We all make little mistakes when we're frustrated," Mom Shelby says.

"I wonder if he'll want to read with me again."

"Sure. This time maybe it would be best to follow along with his interests if you can't interest him in yours."

"You're right. Next time I will like green eggs and ham. I will like them Sam I am," Dad Shelby quips.

Second Chance: Turn to Scene 167

RESPECT FOR SELF AND OTHERS CASE STUDY 3: Cat Has Children's Tongue

"Wow! My call to Mr. Carlson backfired," mutters Mom Shelby.

"It sure did. Most people wouldn't like to hear over the phone that their cat was drowned in a bag by the neighbor's children. I guess Mr. Carlson isn't an exception," observes Dad Shelby.

RESPECT FOR SELF AND OTHERS

"I had hoped talking honestly to Mr. Carlson would calm him down. I guess I was hoping for too much. How else could I have handled it?"

"To be honest, I would have let the cat stay buried and said nothing. Not that I think that silence would be right. I just don't think Mr. Carlson's knowing how his cat died would do any good. Let's ask Ken West. He's the author," suggests Dad Shelby.

"Leave me out of this one! This is one of the toughest cases in the book," pleads Ken West.

"Exactly. That's why I want your opinion. You got us into this," insists Dad Shelby.

Unable to squirm his way out of the request, the author begins, *"First, I want to commend Mom Shelby for the way she handled the situation. You confronted your children and were open and honest with Mr. Carlson. You showed courage calling a neighbor who isn't the biggest fan of children. Even Dad Shelby's solution — not to say anything — has its advantages. But I'm not sure that avoiding the truth is a good way to teach children that **lying** isn't right."*

"Speaking of avoidance, why do I have the feeling you're sidestepping answering my question?" Dad Shelby interjects.

"I'm trying to say that some problems have no single, right answer. At best, we can talk about possible solutions and choose the one we believe may be best. Another possibility? How do you think it would have worked to have the children talk to the Carlsons? Of course, you could have practiced with them beforehand and accompanied them to offer support," Ken West suggests.

Somewhat astonished, Mom Shelby considers the option, then replies, *"I'm really not sure. I would have been terrified at the prospect of what Mr. Carlson might say to them. Of course, I would never let him do anything to them. The best that could happen is that they would really learn about taking responsibility for their behavior. I guess they'd learn something about courage too."*

"What's the worst that could happen?" asks Ken West.

"I suppose Mr. Carlson could berate them and insist that we whip the children right then and there," Mom Shelby answers.

"How would you and the children handle that?" Dad Shelby wonders.

*"Of course, I wouldn't let Mr. Carlson touch my children. As far as verbal abuse, that depends on how awful he was being. I believe we could handle almost anything. I could prepare the children for the worst. After all, who could blame Mr. Carlson for being emotional? If he lost control, we could walk away from his **temper tantrum**,"* Mom Shelby says.

"Sounds as if your family can handle anything as long as you stick together in a crisis," Ken West observes.

"I think you're right. Of course, I'm not positive what I would do if I were in the situation again, but I think I would have the children talk with Mr. Carlson, as long as I could prepare them for it. Maybe the reader will give me that chance," Mom Shelby hopes.

Second Chance: Turn to Scene 93

244

Revenge

After all I have done for you, how could you treat me this way? If this has ever been a thought of yours, then you understand revenge. Revenge is the first of the two perilous **goals** of misbehavior.

All children will occasionally be angry or hurt after losing a power struggle with a parent and may attempt to "get back" by hurting them. These occasions should be rare. But if parents are frequently hurt by their child, then something may be seriously wrong with the relationship.

What is wrong is that the child is feeling defeated and hurt. Feeling overwhelmed and unable to win against the parents or others, on any terms, causes the child to feel unloved. Still having some spirit, the child attempts to return the hurt. It is a clear case of revenge: "I am hurt, and I will hurt you in return."

Parents need to be mature and break the cycle of revenge, even though they themselves may feel hurt and angry. Most importantly, children need to learn that their parents love them. **Communicate** your positive feelings assertively. Spend time with your child. Pursue activities your child enjoys. **Encourage** your children and withhold criticism.

If revenge has become a predictable pattern within the family, seek **family therapy.** Revenge is a serious goal and parents usually need professional help in breaking the cycle. "More of the same" never works. Professional help can bring better days to your family.

REVENGE CASE STUDY: Massacre at Broken Vase

"This was the worst morning of my life," declares Mom Shelby. "Wendy refused to dress, then hit me when I tried to dress her. Then she knocked over my prized vase. How could she treat me this way after all I've done for her!"

"The worst part seemed to be when you chased her to the bus stop, and she ran into the street in front of that car," observes Dad Shelby.

With tears welling, Mom Shelby sighs, "Everything I did backfired. I was so hurt and angry. But when Wendy was almost run over by the car, I just lost control inside. I've never been so frightened."

"Wendy must have been upset to hit you and break your vase." Dad Shelby sidesteps Mom Shelby's emotions.

*"I guess so. We had one of our outrageous **power struggles**. I know I should avoid them, but when Wendy escalated her misbehavior, so did I. She beat me in the end. Actually, she devastated me," confesses Mom Shelby.*

"Sounds more like she hurt you. Breaking the vase was a desperate act of revenge."

"She hurt me so badly. I just wanted to lash out at her."

"You did. Things just got worse and worse. It's amazing how a simple power struggle can accelerate out of control," Dad Shelby observes.

"Yes. We both lost our composure. I guess the difference is that she's a child. I should have realized that I was making things worse by charging after her. Someone had to stop the cycle of hurt."

"I agree. But it's easier to understand that after the emotions die down."

"Next time, I will know better. You can't imagine how frightened I was. I swear I'll never let things rage out of control that badly again. I've learned my lesson."

Second Chance: Turn to Scene 1

Routines

Routines are as important to children as skeletons are to the body. Routines offer children structure, security, and boundaries. Particularly important to young children's daily lives, for example, are consistent bedtime routines. When routines are suddenly broken, children may experience difficulty going to sleep and as a consequence may be irritable and difficult to manage the next day.

After routines are broken, several days may be required to retrain a child. Following long trips or visits to grandparents, adults frequently must invest time in retraining children. Divorced parents also face predictable challenges in reestablishing routines following periods of visitation.

Children and teenagers will push the limits to try to break routines. However, routines are helpful to people of all ages. Teenagers need limits as much as young children do. Good routines will change with age and will not be too rigid to allow important exceptions.

Busy parents benefit from routines as do their children. When children know that their parents will spend time with them at a designated time each day, they become more patient. Patience helps everyone when adults are trying to prepare supper or regain their balance after a challenging day.

Show **respect for yourself and others** when deciding whether or not to break a child's routine. When parents break routines for the wrong reasons, the resulting benefits seldom outweigh the sticky complications.

ROUTINES CASE STUDY 1: Takes a Brat to Know a Brat

"Why did you decide that you were not going to read to Wally? You know how important his routine is," asks Mom Shelby.

"I haven't had a single minute to myself today. I deserve my own private time," Dad Shelby explodes.

"Yes, you do. And, Wally deserves his routine. You know that Wally needs his routine to go to sleep or he will create major headaches for all of us. When his routine is broken, we all suffer."

"So, you're saying I have to give in."

"No. Talk with me. Believe me, I understand not having any personal time. If I had known how frustrated you felt, I could have read to Wally. Or, we could have split the reading," Mom Shelby replies.

"But that's not fair to you. I didn't want to cause trouble for you," Dad Shelby says.

"You've got to be kidding. Whenever a child's routine is smashed, adults pay a stiff price. This is a perfect example. How much have you enjoyed your private time?" Mom Shelby asks.

"What private time? I've spent the entire night listening to Wally whine and talking with you."

"Exactly! Routines save time in the long run. Never break a bedtime routine unless you're prepared to pay for it the rest of the night. Next time let's work on communications. We can work things out in advance. But after the damage is done, we all suffer."

"No kidding. This is one lesson I will remember," vows Dad Shelby.

Second Chance: Turn to Scene 181

ROUTINES CASE STUDY 2: The Stolen Binky Caper

"I should have saved the Binky-breaking for another night," admits Mom Shelby.

"What do you mean?" asks Dad Shelby.

"Wally's too dependent on his blanket for me to take it away from him suddenly."

"You didn't take it away. Wendy hid it."

"True. And her trick just made the situation worse. Wally felt mistreated by Wendy, then betrayed by me. I'll need to remove the Binky the old fashioned way — piece by piece. We'll cut off a little of the blanket each day until it disappears. First, however, I need to set up a plan with Wally in advance. No surprises," says Mom Shelby.

"Why don't you create a **contingency**? When he gives up his Binky, let him do something he's looking forward to," suggests Dad Shelby.

"That might work. Maybe I'll offer Wally the choice of how to separate from his Binky."

"Or, you could just announce that next week you'll take away his Binky completely. People shouldn't be so dependent," suggests Dad Shelby.

"What if I took away your favorite feather pillow — the one you take on business trips and vacations."

"That's different. I need that pillow to sleep well at night," explains Dad Shelby.

"Just like Wally needs his Binky. Completely taking away his blanket might work, but I think I'll use a softer approach. I tried the cold turkey technique tonight and my turkey got cooked!" quips Mom Shelby.

"You've got a point. Sometimes slower is better," agrees Dad Shelby.

"I'll wait to create a plan with Wally tomorrow when he's not so tired. I just wish I had been more sensitive tonight."

Second Chance: Turn to Scene 171

ROUTINES CASE STUDY 3: Called from Routine

"But the phone call could have been important," Dad Shelby mounts his defense.

"Reading to Wally is important. Other people can wait," replies Mom Shelby.

"What if the call had been an emergency?"

"The caller would have told us, and one of us could have taken over while you talked. William loves to read to Wally for short periods. Could it be that you didn't really want to read?" Mom Shelby probes.

"I guess I didn't. I'm really tired. I was hoping that when I returned from the call Wally would be asleep," admits Dad Shelby.

"That sounds like William when he avoids taking out the trash and hopes that we won't notice," laughs Mom Shelby.

"I guess so. A job is a job. I tried to finesse Wally, but it's almost impossible to sidestep an almost-five-year-old."

"You're absolutely right. We need to put first things first. Routines are usually more important than interruptions prove to be. In fact, this five minute interruption kept Wally up for an extra hour. He'll be in a foul mood tomorrow. Most of the time it's easier to stick to the routine and get the job done."

Second Chance: Turn to Scene 169

ROUTINES CASE STUDY 4: Sugar-Charged Bedtime

"Nothing makes me more angry than for you to get the kids riled up and wide awake at bedtime — then leave them for me to put to sleep!" shouts Mom Shelby.

"I just wanted to do something fun. Eating cookies with Wally seemed like a good idea," Dad Shelby replies.

"How many times must we go through this? It's always something. You watch an exciting movie with them or tickle them or give them candy. Then you escape to your workroom, and I have an excited child on my hands. Why do you keep on doing this to me?"

"What do you want me to say — that I'm an idiot who fails to learn from experience?"

"That will do fine! I agree." laughs Mom Shelby

"I swear I'll never do this again," promises Dad Shelby.

*"If you do, you'll have to accept the **logical consequences** and stay with the children until they go to sleep," promises Mom Shelby.*

"Okay. I get the point. Next time, I'll stick to the routine. Breaking it is beginning to cause me more problems than it's worth."

Second Chance: Turn to Scene 165

S

Self-Esteem

My favorite definition of self-esteem is based on the gap between who children believe they should be and who they believe they are. The smaller the gap, the greater the self-esteem. Therefore, children who appear to be extremely successful can be plagued by low self-esteem if their immediate goals far exceed their performance. Also children with modest accomplishments can be quite confident and pleased with themselves. In other words, the gap is narrow between who they believe they should be and who they are.

Encouragement is the key to building positive self-esteem. Techniques that make children feel as if they're not succeeding in life create discouragement and low self-esteem.

Four Horsemen of Low Self-Esteem

- *focusing on mistakes* — apparently, some parents and teachers are cursed by the need to always look at the negative. Instead of commenting on the good grades on a report card, they talk only of the bad marks. Rather than applauding children for setting the table or cleaning the kitchen, they point to the shortcomings of their efforts. When overly criticized, children learn that they "can't do anything right." Use encouragement. Children flourish when parents focus on successes rather than accentuate their failures.

- *perfectionism* — because of their own lack of self-esteem, many adults frantically seek a **utopia** where they can exist above all criticism. Perfectionists' children may be doomed to feel as if a critic is always looking over their shoulder and always ready to criticize. Perfectionists limit their worlds severely. They tend to avoid novelty or challenges that may lead to errors and feelings of humiliation. Allow children to be children. They need to explore, try new activities, and fly on their own. To do so, they cannot be afraid to make a mistake.

- *comparisons* — although comparisons usually are made to motivate children, these good intentions almost always backfire. Comparisons always assure a child that the gap is wide between who he should be and who he is: "Why can't you be as good in math as your brother?" "You're not living up to your test scores." (This comparison literally means that you're not as good as yourself.) Parents hate to be compared: "Why aren't you as nice as Tommy's mother?" "Our teacher last year told better stories than you do." Eliminate comparisons.

- *neglect* — some adults fail to support children at home or in school. Adults may neglect to take an interest in their children's school work. Or, they may not **communicate** their love and appreciation. Neglecting a child in any area creates conditions that foster low self-esteem. Take an interest in your child's life. Communicate the positive as well as negative. Be active.

The Shelbys:

"I thought that only people who were doing poorly in school or at work suffered from poor self-esteem," admits Dad Shelby.

"No. I can see low self-esteem in some of my best students," observes Mom Shelby. "They become frantic and depressed if they don't make A's on their tests or projects."

"In other words, if they don't do perfectly they feel as if they have failed," Dad Shelby concludes.

"That's exactly right. In fact, some of my best students seem anxious and tense. They put tough 'shoulds' on themselves: 'I should do perfectly on everything all of the time,'" Mom Shelby continues.

"I suppose if your goal is perfection, you will always be at risk for creating a gap between who you are and who you believe you should be," Dad Shelby infers.

"That's really true. It seems as if my students with low self-esteem either give up or create tyrannical expectations," explains Mom Shelby.

"Neither choice seems good to me," asserts Dad Shelby.

"Neither extreme is fun to teach. Both groups are discouraged much of the time. It's tough to have to prove your worth on every test or exam or when every evaluation confirms you're not everything you believe you should be," Mom Shelby sadly observes.

Stealing

Young children do not possess a firm sense of the meaning of personal property. As with **lying** and **cheating**, when children steal, parents should not overreact. A theft does not represent a character failure. Children's morality requires years to mature.

Making restitution provides an important learning experience for young children. Have children return stolen property to the rightful owner. Facing the victim of the theft makes a permanent impression and allows children to develop an appreciation for the concept of personal property. Also, by personally restoring the stolen item, children learn to accept the **logical consequences** of their own behavior.

When children become preteens and teenagers, the reasons for stealing become more complicated. Some steal for excitement, others enjoy attention from peers, and a few choose to match wits with adults. If stealing becomes frequent, then parents need to seek outside help. A pattern of theft suggests that serious problems exist.

Be sure that your family **values** are clear. A few parents believe stealing in specific situations is fine. For example, not reporting all of one's income for tax purposes sends a message to children that "getting away" with crime can be acceptable. On the other hand, if children consistently violate the values of their family, **family therapy** can help create solutions.

STEALING CASE STUDY: Caught Chocolate-handed!

"The clerk at the store was a jerk. So Wally stole some candy bars. Big deal. Every kid steals something some time. Why did the clerk have to pick a fight with me?" wonders Dad Shelby.

"Why did you take over the situation? It sounds as if the children were handling the problem with the clerk quite nicely," observes Mom Shelby.

"I took over because I'm Wally's father. It's up to me to straighten out these messes."

"It seems as if you made more of a mess. Why didn't you watch to see how the clerk and the kids would handle things? It was their problem, not yours."

"Do you think they could have worked things out?" asks Dad Shelby.

"Yes, I do. Most clerks are accustomed to dealing with this type of problem without going overboard. But you could always have intervened if the clerk had become unreasonable," Mom Shelby answers.

*"You're right. I should have let them accept their own **logical consequences.** Sometimes I take over when I should allow others to handle their own problems. I like to feel in control."*

*"That's natural. You handle crises extremely well, and you like to be helpful. But the children need to learn to be as good in a crisis as you are. They can only become that good with practice. You need to show **respect for yourself and others**. Particularly, you need to respect your children's ability to handle tough situations," suggests Mom Shelby.*

"I have to admit that they could have done as good a job as I did. I'm sure they would have worked out something with the clerk. Wally would probably have ended up paying the

clerk back eventually. I'm afraid that things grew worse the second I jumped into the situation," says Dad Shelby.

"When you jumped in, you landed with both feet on top of a delicate situation. Still, I'm glad you were near in case the children needed help. I just wish you had shown more confidence in them."

"Next time I will. Children are always more resourceful than I give them credit for being."

Second Chance: Turn to Scene 68

Swearing

Curse words leak into every household. Initially, preschool children will repeat words they've overheard. Usually the meaning of the words is unknown, but children are impressed with the reactions the words ignite.

When a child first experiments with cursing, explain in simple terms why cursing is not allowed: "There are some words that make people feel good and some words that make people feel bad. This is one that makes people feel bad."

The next time the curse word is used, use a **logical consequence.** For example, **quality time out** usually works well. Incidentally, if a parent curses, the same consequences should be followed that are required for the child.

Never allow cursing to become a weapon the child knows will rattle parents. If cursing is treated as no big deal and reasonable consequences are built in, then cursing seldom becomes a problem.

The Shelbys:

"For once, we did things perfectly!" announces Dad Shelby.

"I bet I know the very incident you're thinking about," agrees Mom Shelby.

"You probably do. We all agreed that anyone who curses must go to his or her bedroom for five minutes. William spent a considerable amount of time there during the first week he rode the bus to school," Dad Shelby reminisces.

"And then there was the Super Bowl. Your team was about to score with two minutes left. Bam! A hard tackle and the ball was fumbled. And what did you say?"

"All I'll confess is that the word has four letters and slipped out loudly. William looked straight into my eyes and said, 'That will be five minutes, Dad.' I was really proud of him," Dad Shelby crows.

"And I was proud of you for actually going to your room and missing the next five minutes."

"Of course, all I missed was five minutes of commercials! But I did go to my room. After that, we seemed to have much less trouble with cursing."

"Maybe that's because your team never made it to the Super Bowl again!" laughs Mom Shelby.

T

Temper Tantrums

Every parent knows about temper tantrums. Some tantrums erupt because of frustration. At other times, tantrums are carefully calculated. Children quickly discover what effect their tantrums have on others.

Permissive parents reward tantrum-throwers by giving in to their displays. As a result, children use emotional blackmail frequently to demand what they want when they want it. On the other hand, parents with a high need for control may challenge tantrums and create destructive **power struggles.** Neither of these parental reactions proves to be beneficial.

Parents need to teach their children good **communication** techniques. Being frustrated or angry is O.K., but tantrums are an unacceptable way to express these emotions.

When children throw tantrums rather than communicate their emotions maturely, parents should neither give in nor resort to combat. Walking away from the tantrum usually works. Because most tantrums are thrown to force parental involvement, when parents walk away children usually abandon their show. This technique works as well with teenagers as it does with two-year-olds.

Also, parents can create boundaries by announcing, "I will talk with you when you use your eight-year-old voice, but not when you use your two-year-old voice." In addition, parents may be successful in using quality time out when children lose control of their emotions. Don't allow temper tantrums to become a way of life. Teach children and spouses how to express their emotions in acceptable ways.

The Shelbys:

"Why did Ken West add 'and spouses'?" Dad Shelby wonders aloud.

"Gosh, I'm sure I wouldn't know. Maybe spouses tend to have tantrums when things

aren't going their way. You wouldn't know anything about that would you, dear?" Mom Shelby inquires with a touch of sarcasm.

"Don't start in on me. I do not have tantrums. I just express my emotions loudly. There's a difference."

"What's the difference, sweetheart? I'm sure your anger looks like a tantrum to the children. It certainly looks that way to me," says Mom Shelby.

"I do not throw tantrums! Do you hear me? I do not throw tantrums!" screams Dad Shelby, as he pounds the table for emphasis.

Mom Shelby walks away and into the living room.

"Come back here and admit it. I do not throw temper tantrums," yells Dad Shelby. Mom Shelby doesn't return. Dad Shelby thinks for a moment, smiles, then mumbles: "Well, at least I don't drop to the floor and beat the tiles with my fists."

u

Utopia

Perfectionists dream of utopia but usually create stress, and they can place their children's **self-esteem** at risk. Perfectionism tends to run in families. The condition is resistant to change because it is not without benefits. Perfectionists usually thrive in school and perform well in society. Although they may complain about their "condition," perfectionists' confessions usually seem more like boasts.

There is nothing wrong with perfectionism unless the practice creates problems for people. Because utopia is impossible to reach, perfectionism always ends in failure. Living is a very risky adventure. If we attempt to develop our potential fully, we will make mistakes. Rudolf Dreikurs believed that to live well we must develop the "courage to be imperfect."

When adult perfectionism leads to a consistent dose of criticism for children, then young people's self-esteem can be threatened. Children soon begin to believe that nothing they do is good enough. As adults they recall, "I could never really please my parents." To protect themselves, children who live with constant fault-finders either declare **inadequacy** by totally giving up or they become perfectionists in an attempt to reach a criticism-free utopia.

Parents need to develop the courage to be imperfect. Ask children to help you understand something they do well. Admit errors. Try challenges that will not be met with total success. Focus on the child's effort and intentions rather than the result. For instance, it is more helpful to say, "I'm pleased you enjoy history and social studies," than to announce "I'm proud that you made A's on your report card."

The Shelbys:

"*Goofing makes all the difference in the world in my classes,*" *Mom Shelby acknowledges.*

"*What do you mean?*" *asks Dad Shelby.*

"*When I make a mistake and say, 'I goofed,' the children laugh. They don't laugh at me, rather they seem to be relieved. Because I admit my mistakes, my students seem to be more willing to take chances.*"

"*I agree with your students. In fact, I work best in an atmosphere where people try their best but mistakes are not viewed as catastrophic,*" *Dad Shelby agrees.* "*Maybe that's the way we should treat our living room,*" *adds Dad Shelby.*

"*What are you getting at?*" *Mom Shelby asks with a certain tinge of suspicion.*

"*I think we all feel more anxious at home because we insist that the entire house must be perfectly clean all of the time.*"

"*I have a feeling that your word 'we' is really 'you,'*" *Mom Shelby assumes.* "*But I get your point. Sometimes I'm so caught up in wanting the house to look perfect that I don't really have fun with the kids.*"

"*It's not just your problem. Sometimes the children seem tense. The more you warn Wally not to spill anything, the clumsier he becomes.*"

"*Okay. You're right. I'm going to develop the 'courage to be imperfect,'*" *Mom Shelby declares.*

"*Yep. And, I bet you'll develop it perfectly,*" *smiles Dad Shelby.*

Values

Family values exist only when both parents declare that something is important and both parents provide a model. In other words, both parents must "talk the talk and walk the walk." When parents provide a clear family value, then all children usually adopt that belief no matter what their **ordinal position** may be.

Most families have fewer family values than they realize. For example, for parents to hold a true family value for education, both must not only talk about the importance of education but also model its value. Children will learn more from watching what their parents *do*. After dinner if one parent reads while children do **homework** and the other parent watches an endless series of television shows, then one adult models the benefits of education and the second does not. No clear family value for education exists. As a result, one child may model after the intellectually active parent and another may seek the comforts of television.

Parents need to talk about the values they wish to teach, but remember, children are impressed more by what parents do than by what they say.

VALUES CASE STUDY: Ambushed!

"Now I know how General Custer felt at Little Big Horn," Dad Shelby announces.

"I guess you felt attacked. I know you were looking forward to the big game, but William needed to do his homework. The children will watch television until their eyeballs bounce off the walls," explains Mom Shelby.

"I just wanted to see basketballs bounce off the hardwood. Why didn't you talk with me in advance? I could have gone over to Uncle William's house or made other arrangements."

"I didn't anticipate this crisis. Besides, we need to support our children's schoolwork. Television is eating away their time and grades. We need a family value that includes no television for the children until homework is completed. In fact, maybe you and I should join them in a quiet time with no television," Mom Shelby pushes.

"Did you read what Ken West wrote above this dialogue? Family values mean that both parents must agree and model the value. You did not ask for my agreement," huffs Dad Shelby.

"You're right. But there was no time, and I was exasperated."

*"You wasted more time by not **communicating** than you saved by acting on your own. Next time, pull me aside. Let's talk," suggests Dad Shelby.*

*"You're right. In fact, let's set up a time now to talk about values. We need to present a united front about the importance of homework and education. Maybe after we talk, we could have a **family meeting** and allow the children to select a limited number of shows," suggests Mom Shelby.*

"Fine, except for sports. I need to watch sports."

"I suppose we really need to talk," sighs Mom Shelby.

Second Chance: Turn to Scene 129

W

Waking/Sleeping

Nothing is more important than **routines** in establishing good sleeping habits. Habits that help children to become independent or "self-soothers" work best.

One of four infants develops sleep problems, according to researchers. Problems occur more frequently with children whose parents become part of their going-to-sleep routine. When children who are rocked to sleep or whose parents stay in the room as they go to sleep awaken in the night, they need their parents' presence to return to sleep. The parents' active involvement becomes part of their children's sleep habits.

Children tend to return to sleep more easily during the night when their parents follow a nightly ritual. After bathing and talking to their children, parents need to leave the room to allow babies (six months of age and over) to go to sleep on their own. Children and adults awaken several times each night. Those accustomed to going to sleep on their own become self-soothers and are able to return to sleep without help. If sleep problems have already developed, consult your physician for retraining tips.

As children become older, place them in charge of their waking and sleeping. When youngsters understand time, teach them to use an alarm clock. After your nightly ritual, allow them to put themselves to sleep with the agreement that they must be able to wake themselves when the alarm sounds. If they fail to awaken on their own, take charge of their bedtime the next evening. Then offer them another opportunity to be in charge the next night.

Parents frequently struggle to regain lost routines. Sleep is self-rewarding. The key to returning children to a schedule is to wake them early in the morning. When bedtime arrives they will be tired. Parents are less successful when they force children who are not tired to go to bed earlier in the evening.

Tips That Make Sleep Routines Easier

- Avoid allowing children to develop troublesome habits, such as going to sleep in their parents' bed. (Clearly an exception occurs for parents who want their children to sleep with them for philosophical reasons.)

- Avoid allowing children to watch television immediately before bedtime.

- Avoid giving children long naps or late naps if they are experiencing sleep difficulties.

- Avoid giving children sugar-laden snacks before bedtime.

- Avoid breaking routines except under exceptional circumstances.

The Shelbys:

"Developing good sleeping routines is mostly common sense," observes Mom Shelby.

"I agree. But why didn't we have a good grasp of the obvious? We let Wendy sleep in our bed, and it took months to return her to her own room," recalls Dad Shelby.

"Our mistake occurred because we were so exhausted. It was easier to let her sleep with us."

"It was easier at the time, but the price we paid in the long run was heavy. I couldn't sleep with her in the bed, not to mention ... well, you know," Dad Shelby says with a certain amount of embarrassment.

"I know. Our intimacy was nonexistent during the weeks she stayed with us. Bad habits are easy to create but hard to break," Mom Shelby confesses.

"Mark Twain was right: 'When it comes to trouble, it's easier to stay out than to get out.'"

Xylophones and Lessons

Children need opportunities to explore their interests and to develop potential. Parents tend to employ different strategies after their children lose interest in a sport or instrument. Some force children to stick to the activity. As a result, **power struggles** frequently follow. Other parents allow children to redirect their interests.

Neither approach is entirely right or wrong. However, allowing children to follow their interests offers more opportunities for them to discover their true loves and talents. Childhood should be a time for experimentation. When a particular sport or musical instrument provides more irritation than pleasure, changes should be allowed. Of course, most parents ask children to honor their commitments to teams or teachers before taking up another activity.

Children can become overloaded quickly with extracurricular events. If your children show signs of stress, be sure that they're not being overwhelmed with commitments. Time to play with friends and to be alone are important to people of all ages.

The Shelbys:

"That message does not help me at all," Mom Shelby exclaims.

"You must be talking about William's violin lessons," concludes Dad Shelby.

"You're darn right I am. William has been taking lessons for three years and he's good. I think we should force him to continue. Some day he'll thank us," explains Mom Shelby.

"Maybe. But right now all you do is fight with him about practicing. The more you fight, the more he hates playing, and the sicker I grow of the entire mess."

"But if he quits, what will we be teaching him? He'll learn not to follow through with commitments unless they're totally fun."

"Or maybe he'll find an interest that he loves. It seems to me as if you're more interested in his violin success than he is," suggests Dad Shelby.

"That's not true. Well, I guess it is true. But at his age how is he supposed to know what's important?" Mom Shelby asks.

*"He knows what's important to him right now. And so do I. These constant **power struggles** over lessons and practice drive me wild. I'd rather enjoy positive relationships than endure this constant fighting,"* replies Dad Shelby.

"I'm still not convinced. Let's talk about it later. I wish the solution to this problem were simpler," Mom Shelby complains.

"Maybe the solution will seem simpler after your next fight with William!" Dad Shelby predicts.

Yahweh and Religion

Sharing your religious beliefs and **values** is important to children's growth. Realize that children's religious thinking develops slowly. Young children are literal thinkers. They believe stories occurred exactly the way they hear them.

Children are unable to understand complex religious ideas. A full appreciation of symbolism is not achieved until their teenage years or young adulthood. Therefore, children are uninterested in complicated sermons or lessons.

A child's simplicity of faith and belief can be refreshing and enjoyable. However, the value of their faith in helping them to deal with crises in life should never be underestimated.

The Shelbys:

"Do you remember when one of the babysitters told William not to be afraid at night because the Holy Ghost was always watching over him?" asks Mom Shelby.

"Do I ever. William was afraid all night. He thought a ghost was in his room," recalls Dad Shelby.

"People sometimes don't understand how children think. Sometimes the assistant minister in church delivers a children's sermon that I don't even understand," admits Mom Shelby.

"Yes. Then he complains that the children are not paying attention. He thinks it's their fault they're restless," notes Dad Shelby.

"The real problem is that his message flies over their heads and they become bored."

"Sometimes I wish I could go back to childhood," Dad Shelby reflects.

"Why?" asks Mom Shelby.

"Faith was so simple then. Things become so much more complicated as we grow older."

"That's true. But I guess that's the point. As we grow older we think about religion very differently. When it comes to thinking, adults and children live in different worlds," Mom Shelby says.

"Yes. And adults seem to think about religion in different ways too. Life becomes complicated, doesn't it?" Dad Shelby asks.

"Amen," agrees Mom Shelby.

Z

Zebras and Other Pets

Good Luck! Children usually agree to any terms before bringing a new pet into the home. But after the novelty of owning a pet wears off, parents frequently end up doing most of the work.

At times parents make agreements with children that prove hard to honor. For instance, "If you do not take care of this pet, we will get rid of him." Extreme **consequences** rarely work because adults also become attached to pets.

Good **routines** must be established from the first if children are to be expected to care actively for their pets. Rules, such as "Animals eat before people do," can help. Creating positive routines requires effort on the parents' part. Of course, training children to be responsible requires more time initially than caring for the pets.

Problems usually occur because parents assume the responsibility of taking care of animals rather than expending the effort to train and supervise their children to be responsible. Training works. Remember, if professionals can teach pigeons to play the piano, then parents can train children to walk the dog.

Take time to teach your children. If you fail to, then they will enjoy the family pets and you will take care of them.

The Shelbys:

"*I would get rid of that giant rat in Wendy's room in a heartbeat,*" *proclaims Dad Shelby.*

"*You mean Herman! He's not a rat. Herman is a hamster and he has a wonderful personality,*" *claims Mom Shelby.*

"*Personality! He's more boring than Uncle William. But I admit he might be just as bright,*" *kids Dad Shelby.*

"*You're so mean. You know you love Herman. Now leave him alone,*" *instructs Mom Shelby.*

"*I do leave him alone. You don't. That's the problem. You're taking total care of that stinking pet, and I do mean stinking pet.*"

"*Wendy loves Herman. I don't know why she won't take care of him. But I know she loves him.*"

"*Why should she take care of him? You do. That's easier for her. All she does is play with him. She's not learning about responsibility,*" *Dad Shelby chides.*

"*I suppose you're right. But I cannot let Herman starve.*"

"*Maybe extremes like death don't need to happen. Let's create a new contract in the family meeting. Maybe Wendy shouldn't eat until Herman is fed. But before we can find a solution, you must be willing to stop doing all of the work,*" *suggests Dad Shelby.*

"*Okay. You come up with a plan to present at the family meeting, and I promise to abide by it,*" *Mom Shelby promises.*

"*Good! Now if Wendy would only be as easy to train as Herman is!*"

MORE BOOKS WITH *IMPACT*

We think you will find these Impact Publishers titles of interest:

Teen Esteem
A Self-Direction Manual for Young Adults (2nd Edition)
Pat Palmer, Ed.D., and Melissa Alberti Froehner, B.A.
Softcover: $9.95   112 pages
Without patronizing or lecturing, *Teen Esteem* helps teenagers
develop the skills needed to handle peer pressure, substance
abuse, sexual expression, more. New material on avoiding
violence and healthy ways to deal with anger.

Cool Cats, Calm Kids: *Relaxation and*
Stress Management for Young People
Mary Williams, M.A.
Illustrated by Dianne O'Quinn Burke
Softcover: $8.95   32 pages
Guide to stress management for children 7-12.
Uses "cats" as teachers, illustrating catnaps,

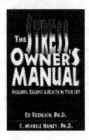

stretching, "hanging in there." Includes section for parents, teachers, and
counselors.

The Child Custody Book
How to Protect Your Children and Win Your Case
Judge James W. Stewart
Softcover: $16.95   192 pages
Explains the process of court child custody litigation,
showing how custody decisions are made, what can be
expected at each stage of the process. Helps eliminate
surprises that could lead to costly mistakes along the way.

The Stress Owner's Manual
Meaning, Balance and Health in Your Life
Ed Boenisch, Ph.D., and C. Michele Haney, Ph.D.
Softcover: $14.95   208 pages
Practical guide to stress management with self-
assessment charts covering people, money, work,
leisure stress areas. Life-changing strategies to
enhance relaxation and serenity.

Impact ✍ Publishers®
POST OFFICE BOX 6016
ATASCADERO, CALIFORNIA 93423-6016

Please see the following page for more books.